CL

1'

0'

india
WITH PASSION

india
WITH PASSION

MODERN REGIONAL HOME FOOD

MANJU MALHI

photographs by Jason Lowe

MITCHELL BEAZLEY

India with Passion
Modern Regional Home Food

First published in Great Britain in 2004 by Mitchell Beazley, an imprint of Octopus Publishing Group Limited, 2–4 Heron Quays, London E14 4JP.
© Octopus Publishing Group Limited 2004
Text © Manju Malhi 2004

A CIP catalogue record for this book is available from the British Library.

ISBN 184 000 947 0

Commissioning Editor: Rebecca Spry
Executive Art Editor: Yasia Williams
Design and Art Direction: Miranda Harvey
Editor: Diona Gregory
Photography: Jason Lowe
Stylist and Home Economist: Sunil Vijayakar
Production: Seyhan Esen
Index: John Noble
Origination: Bright Arts, HK

Printed and bound by Toppan Printing Company in China

contents

The hospitality of Indians is legendary. In Sanskrit literature, *"atithi devo bhava"* means "the guest is truly your god". Indians believe that they are honoured if they share their mealtimes with guests; even the poorest are willing to share their food. This book represents my take on modern Indian home food – whether cooked for the family or for guests. There are no long lists of ingredients or complicated methods, and there's no need for legions of chefs to chop vegetables or pound ingredients for elaborate pastes and spice mixes. This is simply good food, simply prepared using fresh ingredients, designed to accommodate the modern Indian's busy lifestyle.

In compiling these recipes I have had to consider that there is no such thing as "Indian cuisine", but rather there are various "cuisines of India". The scope of Indian cooking is vast and encompasses a wide range of geographic and climatic conditions, centuries of history and many religions and cultures. However, home food is also heavily

introduction
परिचय

influenced by the dishes of restaurants, cafés, and street stalls, so there are plenty of recipes here that have their origins in commercial kitchens.

The art of spicing and choice of ingredients varies from region to region as well as from one cook to the next. Indian food cannot be separated easily from its social and religious context, which is why I have divided this book into regional chapters. India has more languages than any other country, and with 31 states and territories and 15 languages, each spoken in different dialects, it's no wonder that this diverse culture is reflected in the country's cuisines. The states have different climates, enjoy different natural resources, and follow different agricultural patterns. Consequently even the taste, colour, texture, and appearance of the same delicacy changes from state to state.

The two religions that have the most influence on Indian food are Hindu and Muslim. The Hindu vegetarian tradition is widespread in India, although many Hindus eat meat now. Strict vegetarianism is mostly confined to the South and the state of Gujarat in the west. Beef, from the holy cow, is strictly taboo for Hindus, and pork is equally taboo for the Muslims.

India also has an extraordinary ability to absorb and make use of foreign gastronomic influences, and each state has a legacy of foreign influences on its food. Among the most notable are Arabian, Iranian, Mogul, and Chinese. Of these, the Moguls, who invaded India, arguably made the deepest impact. They brought with them exotic spices, dried fruit and nuts. The Indians combined these with milk and cream to make rich Mughlai dishes, including creamy *kormas* and fragrant *biryanis* and *pulaos* (spiced rice dishes). Iranian settlers, known as Parsees, are perhaps best known in culinary terms for their introduction of the "*dhansak*" style of cooking, in which chicken or lamb is cooked with lentils and spices. From the Middle East came new ingredients, such as asafoetida (a dry resin from a tree), pistachio nuts, and coffee, and new ways of cooking, including the *tandoor* (clay oven). The Chinese offered kitchenware such as woks, knives, and plates in return for Indian pepper, and typical Chinese soups, chow meins, chop sueys, and fried rice and vegetables are particularly popular in East India.

Indian cooking combines six basic tastes: sweet, sour, salty, spicy or pungent, bitter, and astringent. A well-balanced Indian meal will contain all six elements. Spices contribute many of the flavours, and the most important spices include chillies, mustard seeds, cumin, turmeric, fenugreek, ginger, coriander, and asafoetida. In sweet dishes, cardamom, cinnamon, nutmeg, and saffron are popular. Besides spices, the main flavouring ingredients are milk and its products, such as yogurt and cream. Onions and garlic are used in many savoury dishes, but they are prohibited in certain Hindu sects. Coconut oil, *ghee* (clarified butter), sesame oil, and mustard oil are the most common cooking oils, although olive oil is used in the Portuguese-influenced Goa region.

Lentils or *dals* are common across the country, although there are regional variations. The word "*dal*" or "*dhal*" denotes not only the ingredient, but also the dish made from it. There are at least five dozen varieties of pulses, the most widely used of which are chickpeas (*kabuli channa*), black lentils (*urad dal*), gram lentils (*channa dal*), red lentils (*masoor*), yellow lentils or pigeon peas (*toor, tuvar* or *arhar*), kidney bean (*rajma*), black-eyed beans (*lobia, rongi* or *chawli*), and mung beans (*green moong dal*). Methods of cooking *dal* vary: in the North *dals* are quite thick, while in the South they have a more soup-like consistency. Some lentils require overnight soaking before cooking, while others can be prepared within minutes.

Indian breads are varied. The simplest bread is the *chapati* or *roti*, which is made from a dough of water and wheat flour and then heated on a griddle or *tawa*. Baste the *chapati* with butter or *ghee* and it becomes a *paratha*. If deep-fried, it is called a *poori* in the North and a *luchi* in the East. Another type of deep-fried bread with a stuffing is the *kachori*. Bake the bread in an oven and it becomes *naan*. And *poppadums* are crispy deep-fried wafers often served with a set meal in a *thali*.

The best Indian rice is the famous basmati. It is predominantly grown in the Dehra Dun Valley, in the foothills of the Himalayas. Served on special occasions, it has long grains, is yellowish in colour, and has a slightly sweet fragrance.

A *thali* is the all-purpose Indian vegetarian dish. Although it belongs to South India, it is found in the West and North too, and there are regional variations. The name comes from the "*thali*" dish in which it is served, which consists of a metal plate with a number of small metal bowls known as *katoris* on it. Sometimes the bowls are replaced by small indentations on the plate itself. Often, the plate is a big banana leaf. The food on a *thali* would be a variety of vegetable curry dishes, relishes, a couple of *poppadums*, *puris* or *chapatis* and a lot of rice. A deluxe variety would include a *pata* (a rolled betel leaf stuffed with fruit and nuts) and may also include yogurt and one or two desserts. The *thali* is replenished with any of the dishes until the eater is satisfied.

Feeling peckish should never be a problem in India, with a wide variety of snack meals and finger foods to choose from. The great snack meal of the South is *masala dosa*, a potato and vegetable curry wrapped in a crispy rice pancake. More portable snacks include *samosas* or *shingaras* (meat or vegetables in a pastry triangle, fried) and *pakoras* (vegetables or potato dipped in chickpea flour batter and deep-fried), which are both found all over India. *Bhelpuris* (puffed rice with tamarind sauce), *panipuris* (the same *puris* filled with a peppery and spicy water), *chana* (spiced chickpeas served with *puris*) and *bhajis* (deep-fried cakes of vegetables in chickpea flour) are also popular in most cities, and are often sold in peddled carts in the night. *Farsans* (crispy spicy fried snacks, like Bombay mix in Britain) can be bought in shops and wayside stalls throughout the country. *Kababs* are common in the North, while *kababs* rolled into griddle-fried bread, known as *kathi* rolls, originated in Kolkata (Calcutta), but are now widely available in other cities.

Milk is the basis for many Indian desserts. *Kheer* (rice pudding), *shahi tukra* (bread pudding), and *seviyan* (vermicelli pudding) are common throughout the country, although *kheer* is called *payasam* in the South. *Kulfi*, a sort of Indian ice-cream, is widely eaten. Milk dishes are usually boiled until the liquid has been removed and then the various ingredients are added to desserts such as *barfi*, which has coconut with almond or pistachio flavouring. Sandesh is a variety of milk dish popular in Calcutta. *Phirni* is a rice pudding dessert with almonds and pistachios. *Bebinca* is a festive favourite in Goa made up of layered pancakes.

India boasts of a wide variety of fruits, from tropical delights in the South to apples, and apricots in the North. Cherries and strawberries are plentiful in Kashmir; mangoes, bananas and melons, particularly watermelons, are widespread; and there are pineapples in Assam, oranges in Kerala, and tangerines in Central India.

Tea is the most popular drink in the North, while southerners prefer to drink coffee. Coconut milk, straight from the young coconut, is a popular street drink, and soda is also widely available. Finally there is the ubiquitous *lassi*, the cool, refreshing, delicious iced yogurt drink.

An Indian meal is rounded off with an after-dinner *paan* – a collection of spices and condiments such as aniseed and cardamom chewed with betel leaves.

India's northerners are a hearty bunch with hearty appetites. Their food is rich, with plenty of cream and warming spices to protect them against the cold climate. In the 13th century the Moguls came through the Himalayan mountains, bringing with them new ingredients, including aromatic spices such as cardamoms and cinnamon bark, and cooking techniques. Some of these techniques were their own, but most were adopted from the Persians, who had a great influence on the Moguls during their journey to India. The distinctive, delicately aromatic flavourings of *pulaos* (spiced rice dishes) and meats cooked with yogurt and fried onions are characteristic of Mughlai food, and the rich curries and *kababs* perfected by the Muslim chefs from Lucknow also have Mughlai influences.

Delhi, the medieval Mogul capital of India, and its surrounding areas of Punjab, the wheat bowl of India, and Kashmir, the jewel of the North, in particular has retained the

north
उत्तर

essence of Mughlai cuisine – a cuisine that the British are familiar with and that is now served up in many Indian restaurants in the western world. With its dairy products, vegetables, lentils and poultry, this is a rich and nutritionally well-balanced cuisine to complement the Punjabi's hard-working lifestyle. Many Punjabis are from a farming background. Wheat is a staple crop, so a variety of breads are cooked in the *tandoor* (clay oven) or a *tawa* (griddle).

The many techniques used in North Indian cooking include braising for dishes such as *korma* and slow oven baking (*dumpukht*). But the *tandoor* and its resulting food, *tandoori*, has achieved popularity the world over. The *tandoor* introduces an earthy flavour to food. The clay oven gets hotter than conventional ovens, so the food is crisp on the outside and moist and tender on the inside, as with *tandoori naan* breads and *tikkas*.

Indeed, the *tandoor* is a social institution. In rural Punjab, the community *tandoor* dug in the ground is a meeting place for the women folk, who bring kneaded *atta* (dough) and marinated meats to have them cooked while chit-chatting. Until a few years ago this phenomenon existed in urban neighborhoods too, but today fewer and fewer have a communal *tandoor*.

The Punjabis have added their own touches to Mughlai dishes, including fragrant spices such as nutmeg and cloves, yogurt, fruit, cream and butter, to create that mellow, slightly nutty flavour that is so typical of Punjabi cuisine. Mention Punjab and the first image that comes to mind is that of lush green fields. Mention Punjabi food and you think of *makke ki roti* (cornmeal unleavened flatbreads) and *sarson ka saag* (mustard leaf spinach). It is simple, sizeable and hearty with absolutely no frills or exotic accompaniments.

In Delhi, cafés and takeaways are influencing modern home-cooking. The city is renowned for its roadside food vendors, *dhabas* (formica-table-topped eateries) and cafés. Once frequented only by truck drivers, today it is in vogue to eat at one of these places, where mouth-watering tandoori chicken, *kababs*, *koftas* (spiced meatballs), *dals* (lentils), *sabzis* (spiced vegetables) and *parathas* (buttered unleavened flatbreads) can be bought.

In contrast to Delhi, Kashmir is a beautiful and serene land, lined with green forests and alpine meadows. Houseboats float on the many breathtaking lakes. On land, fruit orchards lie in abundance. Kashmiri dishes are mild to medium, with highly fragrant, creamy and velvety sauces. Cinnamon, cloves, fennel, cardamom, asafoetida, mace, nutmeg, saffron and chilli are used in abundance along with cream, garlic, tomatoes and capsicums or green peppers.

The cooking is essentially meat-based, with goat's meat or chicken, and the Kashmiri chillies impart a rich red colour to the food. Nuts such as walnuts and dried fruits such as dates and apricots are also used lavishly in puddings, curries and snacks. The main Kashmiri meal is usually followed by a generous serving of fresh fruits such as strawberries, plums, cherries and apples, which only grow in the cool climate of the extreme north of India.

"Land of the great Maharajas", Rajasthan is one of the most colourful and vibrant states in India. It is rich in arts and crafts, culture and a history that dates back over centuries. The granite and marble fortresses and palaces of Jaipur contrast with the vast openness of the *Thar* Desert. The food varies from mild to medium in heat, and the sauces are mainly sweet and creamy in flavour and texture. Coriander, cardamom, turmeric, chilli, cumin and tamarind are widely used. Milk, buttermilk, yogurt, onions, ginger, garlic, green chillies, cashew nuts, mint and jaggery or *gur* (unrefined natural brown sugar) are also used in abundance.

Steam or slow oven baking (*dumpukht*) is inextricably linked with Rajasthan. When the region was constantly locked in battle with neighbouring states, both kings and commoners spent much of their lives in the saddle. Food was on the hoof and outdoor cooking was the order of the day, which is where *dumpukht* comes from. A vessel containing meat and spices was sealed and buried in a pit in the sand, with lighted, dry cowdung below and above it. Gentle heat worked the magic, while the seal kept the flavours in.

In rural Punjab, *al fresco* eating mainly occurs in self-service, roadside food joints called *dhabas*, frequented by truck drivers and travellers. They always serve *dal makhani*, which is cooked on a slow fire, often simmering for hours until the lentils turn creamy and are well flavoured with spices. The *dal* is sometimes rounded off with cream and lashings of butter. A typical Punjabi meal consists of unleavened flatbread or *rotis*, yogurt, curried vegetables, and a lentil dish. *Dals* are a speciality of Punjabi cuisine.

dal makhani
दाल मरूखनी
buttered spiced black lentils

serves 2–3

115g (4oz) whole black lentils
70g (2½oz) butter or *ghee*
pinch of asafoetida (optional)
1 medium onion, finely chopped
2 green finger chillies, finely chopped
2 garlic cloves, finely chopped
¼ tsp salt
½ tsp turmeric

¼ tsp hot chilli powder
1tsp ground coriander
1tsp ground cumin
115g (4oz) cooked kidney beans
1tsp peeled and finely grated root ginger
¼ tsp *garam masala*
2tbsp single cream
handful of coriander leaves, chopped

Check through the black lentils for stones, place in a sieve and wash under cold running water. Soak the lentils in 285ml (½ pint) cold water for 8 hours or overnight. Rinse, then place in a saucepan with 400ml (14fl oz) boiling water. Bring to the boil. Cover and simmer for half an hour, until the lentils are tender.

In a pan, melt 50g (1¾oz) butter. Add the asafoetida and stir. Tip in the onion, chillies, and garlic and gently fry for 7 minutes or until golden, stirring occasionally. Add the salt, turmeric, chilli powder, coriander, and cumin, then the kidney beans (rinsed), lentils and remaining cooking water. Mix and add the ginger. Fry over a medium heat for 5 minutes, stirring occasionally. Add 400ml (14fl oz) boiling water and simmer for 10 minutes. Sprinkle over the *garam masala* and put the remaining butter on top. Swirl in the cream and sprinkle over the coriander.

Punjabis love vegetables and one of their main crops is mustard or *sarson*. The leaves are used to make a special dish known as *sarson ka saag*. This is cooked for hours on a slow fire with minimal spices to retain the fresh flavour of the mustard leaves. *Sarson ka saag* is served with an unleavened cornmeal bread called *makke di roti*. Mustard leaves are not widely available in the West, but mustard seeds are, so I've prepared this hearty green bean and potato dish to celebrate the vigour of the Punjabis.

aloo phalia
आलू फलियां
green beans with potato

serves 2–3

300g (10½oz) dwarf beans, topped and tailed
200g (7oz) white or red potatoes, peeled
¼ tsp mustard seeds
pinch of cumin seeds
2 tbsp vegetable oil
1 medium Spanish onion, finely chopped
1 green finger chilli, finely chopped
¼ tsp turmeric
¼ tsp ground cumin
½ tsp ground coriander
¼ tsp salt
¼ tsp coarsely ground black pepper

Cut the green beans into 5mm (⅕ inch) thick slices. Cut the potatoes into 5mm (⅕ inch) cubes. Heat the mustard and cumin seeds with the oil in a small frying pan. When they start to pop, add the onion and chilli. Fry for a minute, then add the turmeric, ground cumin, coriander, salt, and black pepper, followed by the green beans and potatoes and cook for 2 minutes. Pour in 150ml (5½fl oz) water. Cook over a medium heat for 12–15 minutes. Serve hot with buttered *phulkas* (see page 62).

"*Shahi*" means royal or regal and *Shahi* cuisine is the food of the Mogul kings who conquered parts of India. The distinctive ingredients in *Shahi* dishes are lots of cream, butter, yogurt, and hot spices, such as *garam masala*; milk-based products such as *paneer* also feature strongly.

shahi paneer

शाही पनीर

regal indian cheese

serves 2–3

3tbsp vegetable oil

½tsp cumin seeds

2 black cardamoms, seeds only

1 medium Spanish onion, finely chopped

2 garlic cloves, crushed

1tsp peeled and grated root ginger

2 green finger chillies, finely chopped

200g (7oz) plum tomatoes, blended until smooth

2tbsp natural unsweetened yogurt, whipped until thick

1tsp cornflour

1tsp tomato purée

1tsp demerara sugar

¼tsp salt

pinch of *garam masala*

pinch of medium-hot chilli powder

255g (9oz) *paneer*, cut into 2.5cm (1 inch) cubes

2tbsp double cream

handful of coriander leaves, chopped

Heat the oil in a heavy-based pan, then stir in the cumin and black cardamoms. Fry for 30 seconds, then add the onion, garlic, ginger, and green chillies. Fry for 3 minutes or until the onions are lightly browned. Tip in the tomatoes and cook for 4 minutes or until the sauce is as thick as double cream. Gradually fold in the yogurt. Take the mixture off the heat. Mix the cornflour and 2tbsp cold water to a smooth paste and stir into the onion mixture. Return the pan to the heat. Add the tomato purée, sugar, and 4tbsp cold water, and stir. Tip in the salt, *garam masala*, and chilli powder. Stir in the *paneer* and cook on a low heat for 2 minutes. Swirl in the cream and cook for a minute. Garnish with coriander.

Indian cheese or *paneer* is a must in the vegetarian Punjabi menu. It's a well-known joke that anything made for northerners is always made with full-fat cheese. I have eaten *samosas* that contain *paneer*!

paneer tikka
पनीर टिक्का
indian cheese bites

makes approx 30 cubes

½ tsp *garam masala*

1 tbsp plain flour

½ tsp crushed dried red chillies or hot chilli powder

¼ tsp crushed black peppercorns

2 tsp ground cumin

2 tbsp malt vinegar

½ tsp salt

300g (10½oz) *paneer*, cut into 2cm (⅘ inch) cubes

1 medium Spanish onion, cut into chunks

1 green pepper, deseeded and cut into chunks

2 tbsp vegetable oil

Mix the *garam masala*, flour, chilli, pepper, cumin, vinegar, and salt together. Stir the *paneer* cubes into the marinade, cover and leave for at least 10 minutes in the refrigerator. Soak 5–6 wooden skewers in water for at least 15 minutes. Preheat the oven to 180°C/350°F/gas mark 4 or the grill to medium. Thread the *paneer* on to the skewers, alternating the cheese with chunks of onion and green pepper. Brush with vegetable oil, then roast or grill for 10 minutes, turning occasionally, until the *paneer* is golden yellow. Serve hot with onion salad and *dhania ki chatni* (see page 72).

Paneer is made from whole cow's or buffalo's milk curdled with lemon juice. It is pressed until its texture is firm and similar to tofu. *Paneer* can be diced and sautéed and is used throughout India in a variety of dishes, especially in the north. It's an essential protein source in many vegetarian diets. Chilli *paneer* is the vegetarian version of chilli chicken or barbecued spare ribs.

mirch wali paneer
चिली पनीर
chilli indian cheese

serves 2-3

1tsp cornflour

pinch of salt

1tsp plain flour

225g (8oz) *paneer*, cut into 2cm
(⅘ inch) cubes

3tbsp vegetable oil

2 green finger chillies

1 garlic clove, crushed

1tsp white or demerara sugar

¼ tsp ground black pepper

1tbsp malt vinegar

1tbsp tomato ketchup

1tbsp dark soy sauce

1tbsp hot chilli sauce

1 medium onion, finely sliced into
rings

Mix together the cornflour, salt, and flour with 1tbsp cold water to make a thin
paste. Coat the *paneer* with the paste. Heat the oil in a frying pan and lightly fry
the *paneer* cubes for 5 minutes until golden. Remove with a slotted spoon, drain
on kitchen paper and set aside. In the same frying pan on a low heat, gently fry
the chillies, garlic, sugar, black pepper, vinegar, tomato ketchup, soy, and chilli
sauce with 2tbsp boiling water for a couple of minutes. Add the *paneer* and mix
well, smothering the *paneer* cubes with the sauce. Serve hot in a *phulka* (see
page 62) with onion rings.

Tomatoes were introduced to India by the Europeans and are now a staple ingredient, especially in the North. *Bhunao* (or *bhuna* or *bhuno*) is a method of Indian cooking in which oil or *ghee* is added to a pan, followed by onions, ginger, garlic, and green chillies. After the onions are browned, spices or herbs and often tomatoes are added. Then a small quantity of water, yogurt or stock is introduced to the pan if and when the ingredients start to stick. This recipe uses a similar technique to produce a deliciously spicy *shorba*.

tamatar shorba
टमाटर शोरबा
tomato soup

serves 4

50g (1¾oz) butter or *ghee*
½ tsp cumin seeds
1 medium Spanish onion, finely chopped
115g (4oz) white potatoes, peeled and chopped into 1cm (⅖ inch) cubes
1 garlic clove, crushed
¼ tsp ground coriander
¼ tsp ground ginger
1tsp demerara sugar
¼ tsp salt (optional)
350ml (12fl oz) tomato passata
small handful of coriander leaves, roughly chopped (optional)
4tbsp single cream, to serve (optional)

Melt the butter or *ghee* in a heavy-based pan. Add the cumin seeds. When they splutter, tip in the onion, potatoes, and garlic and fry for 4 minutes. Add the coriander, ginger, sugar, and salt, if using. Mix well and add the passata with 500ml (18fl oz) boiling water. Cover and gently simmer for 5–10 minutes or until the potatoes are tender. Cool, then blitz in a blender until fairly smooth. Gently reheat and serve with a sprinkling of roughly chopped coriander leaves or a swirl of single cream. Offer freshly ground black pepper for extra spice.

Across India, roadside vendors roast corn cobs on hot charcoals or by placing them in hot sand: you cannot avoid the delicious woody aromas wafting across the hustle and bustle of people and traffic. Corn is grown in small inland pockets throughout the country, but the state of Uttar Pradesh is the largest producer. It is harvested from November through to January.

bhutta sika hua
भुट्टा सिका हुआ
roasted corn on the cob

serves 2
2 corn cobs, outer layers removed
knob of butter

pinch of salt
pinch of medium-hot chilli powder
2tsp lemon juice

Place the cobs on a naked flame on a hob or a barbecue. Alternatively, place them under a hot preheated grill. Using tongs, carefully rotate them 4–5 times to make sure they cook evenly. When they are tender and well browned, smear with butter, salt and chilli powder. Finally, sprinkle with the lemon juice and serve immediately.

A typical Punjabi meal consists of *chapatis* or *rotis* baked on a griddle, often some rice, and perhaps a selection of lentil and vegetable dishes with curd or yogurt, and pickles. Punjabi food doesn't appear to be influenced by Kashmiri techniques or Mogul traditions. It's a simple and substantial style of cooking with no frills or fuss.

ghia ki sabzi
घिया की सब्जी
spiced marrow

serves 4

1kg (2lb 3oz) marrow

6tbsp vegetable oil

2 medium Spanish onions, finely chopped

4 green finger chillies, finely chopped

2 garlic cloves, crushed

½ tsp turmeric

½ tsp ground cumin

1tsp ground coriander

½ tsp salt

200g (7oz) tomatoes, finely chopped

1tsp peeled and finely grated root ginger

Top and tail the marrow, then cut it in half, then cut it lengthways and scoop out any seeds. Cut into 3cm (1⅕ inch) pieces. Heat the oil in a heavy-based pan. Add the onions, chillies, and garlic and gently fry for 5 minutes or until golden brown. Add the turmeric, cumin, coriander, and salt. Stir for a minute, then mix in the tomatoes. Cook for a couple of minutes. Tip in the marrow pieces and ginger. Mix well, cover and gently cook for 20 minutes. Serve hot with *phulka* (see page 62) or a *paratha* (see page 58).

Go to any home in the north of India during the winter months and the proverbial *aloo gobhi* will be served at least once a week, either as an accompaniment to a curry or as the main dish with *chapatis*. *Aloo gobhi* is also one of the most popular side dishes served in restaurants in Britain.

aloo gobhi
आलू गोभी
seasoned potato and cauliflower

serves 2–3

200g (7oz) cauliflower florets, cut into 4cm (1⅗ inch) pieces

2tbsp vegetable or groundnut oil

1 large Spanish onion, finely chopped

2 green finger chillies, finely chopped

2 garlic cloves, finely chopped

300g (10½oz) white potatoes, peeled and cut into 2cm (⅘ inch) cubes

1tsp turmeric

¼ tsp ground cumin

¼ tsp ground coriander

½ tsp salt

¼ tsp *garam masala*

1tbsp butter or *ghee*

1tsp peeled and finely grated root ginger

Wash the cauliflower well in salted cold water. Heat the oil in a frying pan and add the onion, chillies, garlic, and potatoes and fry for 7 minutes or until the onion is deep yellow and translucent. Add the cauliflower and fry for a further 3 minutes until light brown. Add the turmeric, cumin, coriander, salt, and *garam masala*, stir and fry gently for 5 minutes. Mix well. Add the butter and mix, then add 5tbsp cold water, cover and simmer for 5 minutes. Stir in the ginger. Serve hot with *phulka* (see page 62) or *dal makhani* (see page 18).

North Indian appetizers or snacks, *Pakoras* are are batter-fried vegetables or fish. The batter is usually made of chickpea or *besan* mixed with water and a few select spices such as coriander and chilli.

gobhi pakoras
गोभी पकोड़ा
cauliflower fritters

serves 2–3

400g (14oz) cauliflower florets, cut into 2.5cm (1 inch) pieces
200g (7oz) chickpea flour
½ tsp coriander seeds, crushed
½ tsp ground cumin
½ tsp salt
½ tsp turmeric
½ tsp medium-hot chilli powder
pinch of baking powder
vegetable oil, for deep-frying

Wash the cauliflower thoroughly in salted cold water. Whisk the chickpea flour and 255ml (9fl oz) cold water with the coriander seeds, cumin, salt, turmeric, chilli powder, and baking powder until it becomes a fairly smooth, runny paste.

Heat the oil in a fryer or wok to 180°C/350°F. To check that the oil is at the right temperature, carefully add a small droplet of batter to the oil. If the batter sizzles, the oil is ready. Tip the cauliflower florets into the batter, coat thoroughly then lift out with a slotted spoon and carefully immerse them in the hot oil. Fry for 3 minutes or until they are golden brown. Remove and drain on kitchen paper. Serve immediately with *pudina ki chatni* (see page 77).

Cabbage in Hindi is *bandh gobhi* and cauliflower is *phool gobhi*. In the north, cabbage is usually prepared with another vegetable, such as potato, and more often than not with lentils. It's also used as a stuffing in recipes that use white bread, such as spicy rissoles. However, this recipe celebrates the cauliflower, which tastes extremely good on its own!

talli gobhi
तली गोभी
fried cauliflower

serves 2–3

500g (1lb 2oz) cauliflower florets, coarsely minced or grated

2tbsp groundnut or vegetable oil

¼ tsp brown or black mustard seeds

1 small Spanish onion, finely chopped

2 medium red chillies, finely chopped

¼ tsp turmeric

¼ tsp ground cumin

¼ tsp salt

Wash the cauliflower thoroughly in plenty of salted cold water. Heat the oil in a frying pan and add the mustard seeds. When they begin to pop, add the onion and chillies. Fry for 1 minute and then stir in the turmeric, cumin, and salt, followed by the cauliflower. Continue gently frying for 10 minutes. Serve immediately with hot *phulka* (see page 62). It is often served with *laal maas* (see page 47).

Kababs are usually made with meat, fish or chicken. These have evolved from the Mogul-style *kababs* and been adapted for the vegetarian market. *"Hara bhara"* means "laden with greens or vegetables".

hara bhara kababs
हरा भरा कबाब
vegetarian kebabs

makes 6–8 *kababs*

115g (4oz) spinach leaves, finely chopped
115g (4oz) white or red potatoes, peeled and boiled
115g (4oz) green peas, cooked
2 green finger chillies, finely chopped
1tsp peeled and finely grated root ginger
½tsp salt
2tbsp roughly chopped coriander leaves
3tbsp cornflour
4tbsp vegetable oil

Wash the spinach thoroughly in salted cold water. In a large bowl, mix together the potatoes, peas, spinach, chillies, ginger, salt, coriander leaves, and cornflour. Mash until fairly smooth. Take a spoonful of mixture, the size of a golf ball, and flatten to make a burger shape. Repeat with the remaining mixture. Heat the oil in a heavy-based frying pan and shallow-fry the patties for 2 minutes on each side, cooking them well. Drain on kitchen paper. Serve hot with *raita* (see page 69).

Though chicken is a favourite with non-vegetarians, fish is also considered a delicacy, especially in the Amritsar region, which is also known for its baked bread made of refined or white flour (*kulcha*). Chunky fish pieces are dipped in a blend of spices and herbs and then deep-fried. It's a kind of Indian-style fish in spicy batter. By the time they've all been fried, they've gone. So make sure you prepare these on your own. So saying, they are an excellent party *hors-d'œuvre* for fish lovers.

amritsari macchi
मच्छी अमृतसरी
amritsari fish

serves 2–3

50g (1¾oz) chickpea or *besan* flour, sifted

1tbsp malt vinegar

1½ tsp hot chilli powder

1 garlic clove, crushed

1tsp peeled and finely grated root ginger

½tsp ajowan seeds

1tsp *garam masala*

½ tsp ground black pepper

½ tsp salt

1tbsp lemon juice

400g (14oz) boneless and skinless cod or sole fillets, in bite-size chunks

vegetable oil, for deep-frying

In a bowl, mix the flour, vinegar, chilli powder, garlic, ginger, ajowan, *garam masala*, black pepper, and salt with about 3tbsp cold water to make a thick smooth batter. Sprinkle the lemon juice over the fish, then place the fish pieces in the batter and mix carefully, ensuring that the fish doesn't break up. Cover and leave to marinate for about 15 minutes.

Heat the oil in a fryer or wok to 180°C/350°F. To check that the oil is at the right temperature, carefully add a small droplet of batter to the oil. If the batter sizzles, the oil is ready. Deep-fry the fish in batches. Cook for 8–10 minutes until golden brown. Drain on kitchen paper and serve immediately with *pudina ki chatni* (see page 77) or *imli ki chatni* (see page 75).

Taken from the ancient *tandoor* cuisine, *tangri kababs* are pieces of chicken marinated in spices and then placed in a clay oven or tandoor. *"Tangri"* means "drumsticks" but I've also included thighs in this recipe.

murgh tangri kababs
मुर्ग टगंडी कबाब
barbecued chicken

serves 4

1kg (2lb 3oz) skinless chicken legs and thighs
juice of ½ lemon
100ml (3½fl oz) natural unsweetened yogurt
4 garlic cloves, crushed
1tsp peeled and finely grated root ginger
1tsp ground coriander
¼ tsp hot chilli powder
1tsp ground cumin
¼ tsp salt

Make two crosswise slits in each chicken piece and rub with lemon juice. Cover and leave for 20 minutes in the refrigerator. In a bowl, mix together the yogurt, garlic, ginger, coriander, chilli powder, cumin, and salt. Add the chicken and mix well, coating all the pieces. Cover and refrigerate for 2–3 hours.

Under a hot grill or on a glowing barbecue, grill the chicken for 15 minutes on each side, until cooked through and golden brown, basting the chicken with a little marinade to prevent it drying out. Serve hot or cold with *phulkas* (see page 62) *pudina ki chatni* (see page 77) and *dal makhani* (see page 18).

The Moguls revolutionized the art of Indian cooking with their *kababs* and *tikkas*: small pieces of meat and vegetables usually cooked on skewers in a *tandoor*. These *kababs* can be served as snacks, starters or even as the main course itself. This recipe is great for barbecues.

murgh seekh kababs
मुर्ग सीख कबाब
spiced chicken kebabs

makes approx 10 *kababs*

1 medium egg

1tsp ground cumin

½ tsp ground white pepper

¼ tsp salt

1tsp hot chilli powder

1tbsp vegetable oil

6–8 ground cashew nuts (optional)

½ small Spanish onion, finely chopped

2tsp peeled and finely grated root ginger

30g (1oz) coriander leaves, chopped

½ tsp *garam masala*

500g (1lb 2oz) chicken meat, minced

vegetable oil, for basting

1 lemon, sliced lengthways into 6

2 medium red onions, finely sliced into rings

Preheat the oven to 180°C/350°C/gas mark 4 or turn the grill on to medium. Soak 10 wooden skewers in cold water for 15 minutes to prevent them burning. In a small bowl, whisk together the egg, cumin, pepper, salt, chilli powder, and vegetable oil. Fold in the cashew nuts (if using), onion, ginger, coriander leaves and *garam masala*. Add this mixture to the chicken and mix well.

Have a bowl of cold water ready for dipping your hands into. With wet hands, pick up a portion of the minced chicken slightly larger than a golf ball and wrap it tightly around each skewer to make a thin sausage shape. Place the skewers directly on the oven shelves or under the grill for 10 minutes on each side, turning and basting them with oil at least twice. Serve hot or cold with lemon slices, onion rings, *anjeer ki chatni* (see page 78) and *khasta roti* (see page 57).

The traditional way of making *tandoori* chicken is by marinating the meat with spices and yogurt and then cooking it in a *tandoor* – a clay pot sunk neck deep in the ground. Charcoal is put inside the pot and heated: it is the heat generated by the hot charcoal that is used for cooking. The meat is pierced on to long iron rods, long enough to reach the bottom of the large clay vessel, and placed inside the pot to cook. These days, you will rarely find *tandoors* in Indian homes but roasting in an oven does provide a similar effect.

murgh tandoori
तंदूरी मुर्ग
whole tandoori chicken

serves 2–3

1 x 1.5kg (3½lb) chicken

4tbsp natural unsweetened yogurt

1tsp *garam masala*

4tbsp single cream

2tbsp medium-hot paprika

1tsp medium-hot chilli powder

1tsp ground cumin

2tbsp lemon juice

2tbsp vegetable oil

1tsp salt

½tsp turmeric

1tbsp tomato purée

4 garlic cloves, crushed

2tsp peeled and finely grated root ginger

Prick the chicken all over and make a few slits about 2cm (⅘ inch) long in the skin. Mix all the remaining ingredients into a smooth paste and smother the marinade generously all over the chicken's skin. Cover and refrigerate for 8 hours or overnight.

Preheat the oven to 180°C/350°F/gas mark 4. Place the chicken in a roasting tin and cover with foil. Roast in the centre of the oven for 1 hour 30 minutes. Halfway through cooking, baste with a little of the marinade. Remove from the oven and leave the chicken in a warm place to rest for 20 minutes. Carve and serve either hot or cold with *khasta roti* (see page 57) or *boondi raita* (see page 69).

Although India's characteristic spices and flavours make excellent soups, Indians are not, on the whole, a nation of great soup eaters. There are, however, some glorious exceptions to the rule, the best known being mulligatawny, the anglicized version of an Indian broth that is British in concept but thoroughly Indian in execution. The Anglo-Indian community has been joyfully wolfing this down for the last 300 years.

mulligatawny
मल्लीगाताउनी
chicken soup

serves 2–3

15g (½oz) butter

1 green finger chilli, slit lengthways

115g (4oz) boneless chicken meat, finely shredded

1tbsp vegetable oil

¼ tsp cumin seeds

2tbsp plain flour

500ml (18fl oz) *murgh ka saalan* (page 66)

¼ tsp salt

2tbsp single cream

30g (1oz) coriander leaves, roughly chopped

Melt the butter in a heavy-based pan and fry the chilli and chicken pieces over a low to medium heat for 10 minutes until the chicken is cooked and lightly browned. Take care not to burn the chilli. Remove the chicken from the pan with a slotted spoon and set aside. Gently heat the vegetable oil in the same pan and add the cumin seeds. When they crackle, add the flour and stir for a minute. Add the cooked chicken, *murgh ka saalan*, and salt. Simmer for 5–10 minutes. Stir in the cream and serve immediately, sprinkled with coriander.

Malai murgh tikka are skewered cubes of boneless chicken cooked in a *tandoor* or clay oven. The unusual ingredient in this recipe is the cheese which adds to the creaminess of the dish. The Nawabs of Oudh – now called Lucknow – in northern India were great gourmets and encouraged their master chefs to innovate and create new styles of cooking. Lucknow and its neighbouring towns were firmly placed on the culinary map thanks to these rich curries, *tikkas*, *kababs*, and breads.

malai murgh tikka
मलाई मुर्ग टिक्का
creamy chicken tikka

serves 2

1tsp lemon juice

¼tsp salt

2 boneless and skinless chicken breasts, approx 310g (11oz), cut into 2cm (⅘ inch) pieces

2tbsp Greek-style natural unsweetened yogurt

30g (1oz) butter

1tbsp double cream

1tbsp *adrak lahsun ka masala* (page 66)

3 green cardamoms, seeds only

½tsp ground cumin

½tsp freshly grated nutmeg

2 green finger chillies, finely chopped

1tbsp groundnut or vegetable oil

2tbsp Cheddar cheese, finely grated

Sprinkle lemon juice and salt over the chicken pieces, cover and set aside. Mix the yogurt, half the butter, the cream, *adrak lahsun ka masala*, cardamoms, cumin, nutmeg, chillies, the oil, and cheese and blend into a smooth paste. Pour over the chicken, making sure it is all well coated, and marinate the meat for 1 hour, covered, in the refrigerator. Soak 4–6 wooden skewers in cold water for 15 minutes to prevent them burning. Skewer the chicken and barbecue, or grill under a preheated grill, for 10 minutes on each side until light brown and cooked through, or simply bake in a preheated 180°C/350°F/gas mark 4 oven for 15 minutes or until the chicken is cooked. Halfway through cooking, baste with the remaining butter (melted). Serve hot or cold on the skewers with *jeera chawal* (see page 56) or *khasta roti* (see page 57).

Shorba is the Indian name for soup. The word *"shorba"* may have been derived from the Moguls, who came into India and influenced this type of dish. There are generally two kinds of soup: the South Indian *rasam* – a consommé-style soup – and the *shorbas* of the North that are creamier and richer in taste. *Shorba* is a thick broth seasoned with mild spices.

masala murgh shorba
मसाला मुर्गे शोरबा
chicken curry soup

serves 2–3

2 tbsp vegetable oil

1 medium onion, finely chopped

1 garlic clove, finely chopped

¼ tsp turmeric

¼ tsp salt

pinch of hot chilli powder

¼ tsp ground cumin

¼ tsp ground coriander

1 tsp tomato purée

1 chicken breast, approx 155g (5½oz), skinned and finely chopped

750ml (26fl oz) *murgh ka saalan* (page 66)

pinch of *garam masala*

1 tsp cornflour

1 tbsp single cream

handful of coriander leaves, roughly chopped

croûtons, to serve

Heat the oil in a heavy-based pan and fry the onion and garlic until they are light golden. Add the turmeric, salt, chilli powder, ground cumin, and ground coriander and stir for a minute. Add the tomato purée, followed by the chicken and fry for 5 minutes to brown the chicken. Pour in the *murgh ka saalan* and sprinkle over the *garam masala*. Cover and simmer for 10 minutes. In a small bowl, mix the cornflour, cream and 1 tbsp cold water to a smooth paste. Add to the pan, mix thoroughly and simmer for another 10 minutes, or until the chicken is cooked through. Serve hot sprinkled with coriander leaves and croûtons.

Black pepper has been exported for centuries and was one of the major attractions for traders-turned-colonists. Peppercorns are the dried berries of the pepper plant, an evergreen creeper. Their heat and pungency make pepper a popular ingredient in curries, *raitas*, *pachadis*, and salads. Peppercorns are also boiled in milk with a pinch of turmeric powder as a remedy for colds and sore throats.

murgh kali mirch
मुर्ग काली मिर्च
black pepper chicken

serves 6

3tbsp vegetable oil

1tsp peeled and finely grated root ginger

2 garlic cloves, crushed

¼ tsp salt

1tsp coarsely ground black pepper

1tsp ground white pepper

6 boneless, skinless chicken breasts, approx 930g (2lb 1oz), cut into bite-size pieces

1 medium onion, finely chopped

2 green finger chillies, slit lengthways

1tsp lemon juice

30g (1oz) coriander leaves, chopped

Mix together 1tbsp of the oil, the ginger, garlic, salt, and the black and white pepper and rub the mixture into the chicken pieces. Cover and refrigerate for at least 30 minutes. Heat the remaining oil in a wok and fry the onion for 2 minutes or until it is translucent. Add the marinated chicken pieces and gently stir-fry for 10 minutes until golden brown. Add the chillies and 200ml (7fl oz) boiling water, cover and simmer for 10 minutes or until the chicken is cooked. To make a thicker or more concentrated sauce, remove the lid to let some of the water evaporate and continue cooking for another 5 minutes. Stir in the lemon juice, and sprinkle over the coriander leaves. Serve hot with *basmati chawal* (see pages 54 and 130) and *aloo gobhi* (see page 30).

There are two main types of cuisines in Rajasthan: Marwari and Rajput. Marwari cuisine is spicy and rich, with an abundance of *ghee*. Rajput food is non-vegetarian and once relied heavily on deer, wild boar, hare, partridge, quail, and sandgrouse. However, with the current hunting restrictions, the Rajasthanis now use goat or lamb; chicken is not popular and fish is never used. *Laal maas* is lamb cooked in garlic, coriander, and enough red chilli to make your hair stand on end. I've used chilli powder instead of the traditional 12–15 dried large red chillies.

laal maas
लाल माँस
hot lamb curry

serves 2–3

500g (1lb 2oz) stewing lamb, cut into 2cm (⅘ inch) cubes
2tsp hot chilli powder
2 garlic cloves, crushed
¼tsp turmeric
½tsp ground coriander

½ large Spanish onion, minced
4tbsp natural unsweetened yogurt
¼tsp salt
2tbsp groundnut oil
1 small onion, fairly thickly sliced
30g (1oz) coriander leaves, roughly chopped

Mix together the lamb, chilli, garlic, turmeric, coriander, minced onion, yogurt, and salt. Cover and marinate for about half an hour in the refrigerator. Heat the oil in a heavy-based pan, add the sliced onion and fry for 4–5 minutes until translucent. Add the lamb and gently cook for 8 minutes, browning the meat. Add 300ml (10½fl oz) boiling water, cover and simmer over a low heat, stirring occasionally, for half an hour or until the meat is tender. Garnish with coriander leaves and serve hot with *khasta roti* (see page 57) or *basmati chawal* (see page 54).

Kakori kababs are soft versions of *seekh kababs*, made with finely ground mince and often a combination of more than 50 spices. Legend has it that Kakori, a small hamlet near Lucknow, is the holy site where millions of pilgrims were fed this offering. A more romantic story associates the *kabab* with the nobility of Avadh, especially the *nawab* who had "aged" before his time and lost the ability to chew: these *kababs* were made to melt in his mouth.

kakori kababs
काकोरी कबाब
lamb kebabs

makes 8–10 *kababs*

4tbsp *channa dal* or Bengal *gram* or yellow split peas

4 green cardamoms, seeds only

1 black cardamom, seeds only

10 peppercorns

2 cloves (optional)

3 dried large red chillies

3tbsp vegetable oil

1 small Spanish onion, finely chopped

500g (1lb 2oz) minced lamb

1tsp salt

¼ tsp freshly grated nutmeg

1 medium egg, beaten

Soak 8–10 wooden skewers in cold water for 15 minutes. Check the *channa dal* for small stones. Heat a small pan and add the *channa dal*, cardamoms, peppercorns, cloves, if using, and red chillies. Roast for 2 minutes, then grind in a coffee mill to a fine powder or use a pestle and mortar. In a frying pan, heat 2tbsp of the oil and fry the onion over a medium heat for 5 minutes until light golden.

Grind the mince into a smooth paste in a food processor with the remaining oil. Add the fried onion, ground spices, salt, nutmeg, and egg. Mix well. Using wet hands, take a golf ball-size lump of the mixture and press it tightly around a skewer in a sausage shape. Repeat with the remaining mince. Place under a preheated grill, or on a barbecue, and cook for 10-15 minutes on each side or until cooked through. Serve hot with *pudina ki chatni* (see page 77).

Awadhi is considered India's most subtle cuisine and is typical of Uttar Pradesh. There are hundreds of varieties of *kababs* such as *kakori kababs, galawat ke kababs, shami kababs,* and *seekh kababs.* "*Galouti*" means "melt in the mouth". The meat was diced, minced, and pounded to a fine paste and then flavoured with herbs and spices. After being moulded into shapes, the *kababs* were grilled, fried, or skewered and baked in a charcoal oven. To achieve the tangy taste, I've used mango powder (*amchur*), but you could use half an unripe mango, finely chopped.

galouti kababs
गलौटि कबाब
cardamom-flavoured lamb patties

makes 4 patties

1tbsp Bengal *gram* or *channa dal* or yellow split peas

255g (9oz) minced lamb, minced several times to make it smooth

1tsp peeled and roughly grated root ginger

2 garlic cloves, crushed

¼tsp mango powder

15g (½oz) butter

1tsp hot chilli powder

2 green cardamoms, seeds only, crushed

½tsp salt

2tsp vegetable oil

1 medium red or white onion, finely sliced, to serve

Pick over the *channa dal* to check for small stones. Place a small pan over a low heat and roast the *channa dal* for 2 minutes, making sure that it doesn't burn. Grind it into a fine powder using a pestle and mortar or coffee grinder. Mix all the ingredients together except the vegetable oil and onion, cover and refrigerate for 2 hours or overnight. Wet your hands and divide the mince into four equal parts. Shape into flat, round patties 1.5cm (⅗ inch) thick.

Heat the oil in a frying pan and shallow-fry the patties over a medium heat, cooking either side for about 10 minutes or until cooked through, making sure both sides brown evenly. Alternatively, preheat a grill to medium and grill for 10 minutes each side or until cooked through. Serve hot with *phulkas (see page 62), imli ki chatni (see page 75),* and onion rings.

The secret of really good *tandoori* cooking lies in the tenderizing, spicing, and marinating of the meat. Lemon juice makes a good tenderizer, but the most commonly used ones are raw papaya, mango, tamarind, yogurt, and sometimes vinegar. Generally, the chops are skewered and then placed in a *tandoor*. The clay oven's wrap-around heat is the ideal method for cooking the chops.

mutton chaap
मटन चाप
lamb chops

serves 3

3 garlic cloves, crushed

2tsp peeled and finely grated root ginger

3tsp lemon juice

½ tsp salt

¼ tsp coarsely ground black pepper

pinch of medium-hot to hot chilli powder

1tsp ground cumin

1tbsp vegetable oil

500g (1lb 2oz) or 6 lamb loin chops

Preheat the oven to 200°C/400°F/gas mark 6. Mix all the ingredients apart from the lamb together in a bowl, then coat the meat well. Lay the chops on a baking tray. Place in the hot oven and roast for 30–35 minutes or until cooked, turning the chops halfway through cooking. Serve hot with *khasta roti* (see page 57) or *jeera chawal* (see page 56) and *boondi raita* (see page 69).

Raan means a leg of lamb marinated in a yogurt-based spice mixture, then roasted on a spit over a wood fire. The recipe has been refined over the centuries and different versions have been created according to the ingredients available, many of which have graced the tables of emperors and maharajas.

raan
रान
marinated roast leg of lamb

serves 4

1.5kg (3½lb) leg of lamb, on the bone

3tbsp vegetable oil

3 garlic cloves, crushed

255ml (9fl oz) natural unsweetened yogurt

1tbsp *garam masala*

1tsp peeled and finely grated root ginger

½tsp salt

¼tsp medium-hot chilli powder

5–6 saffron strands

Prick the flesh of the lamb all over with a skewer. Mix all the remaining ingredients together to make the marinade, and smear it thickly over the lamb. Place on a plate and cover, then leave to marinate in the refrigerator for a couple of hours. Preheat the oven to 180°C/350°F/gas mark 4. Put the lamb in a roasting tin and cover loosely with foil, ensuring that it doesn't touch the lamb. Cook for 2 hours until the meat is tender. Halfway through cooking, baste the lamb with the juices in the pan. Remove the foil and cook the lamb for 8–10 minutes more. Take the meat out of the oven, cover loosely with foil and leave to rest in a warm place for about 15 minutes.

Make a gravy with the remaining juices from the roasting tin by stirring in 75–100ml (2½–3½fl oz) boiling water and simmering over a medium heat for 3 minutes. Carve the lamb and pour the spicy gravy over the meat. Serve with *aloo gobhi* (see page 30), *pudina ki chatni* (see page 77), and *khasta roti* (see page 57).

Basmati is a small but long-grain aromatic rice with a nut-like flavour and aroma. It is always prepared on special occasions. "Basmati" means fragrant and it is the most expensive rice in the world. Originating in South-East Asia, basmati has been cultivated in India and Pakistan for more than 8,000 years. Always rinse the rice thoroughly in cold running water to remove any starchy residue: this makes it less sticky when cooked. A wide variety of rice dishes are made with basmati, such as *pulao, biryanis,* and puddings.

basmati chawal
बासमती चावल
plain basmati rice

serves 2–3

200g (7oz) white basmati rice
¼ tsp salt (optional)
drop of vegetable oil

Rinse the rice for 30 seconds. Place in a saucepan with the salt, if using, and the oil. Add 375ml (13fl oz) boiling water and cover the pan. Simmer on a very low heat for 10 minutes. Remove the lid and, with a fork, check a few of the grains to see if they're cooked. All the water should be absorbed.

Cooled, cooked rice can be stored in the refrigerator for 24 hours only. When reheating rice, warm it in a pan on a very low heat with 1tsp butter or *ghee* or oil. Make sure it is piping hot before serving.

The Punjabis in northern India are predominantly a wheat-eating people, but they cook "seasoned" rice on special occasions. Plain or steamed rice is only eaten when someone is feeling under the weather. Cumin is the second most popular spice in the world after black pepper, and it's also one of the main ingredients in various spice mixtures. The fresh, nutty aroma is unmistakable.

jeera chawal
जीरा चावल
rice with cumin seeds

serves 6
300g (10½oz) white basmati rice
1tbsp vegetable oil
1tsp cumin seeds
¼ tsp salt
15g (½oz) butter or *ghee*

Wash the rice thoroughly under cold running water. Heat the oil in a heavy-based pan. Add the cumin seeds and stir for a few seconds, allowing them to sizzle but not burn. Add the rice and salt. Stir so the oil coats all the rice and it looks glossy. Pour in 600ml (21fl oz) boiling water and add the butter or *ghee*. Cover and simmer on a low heat for 10 minutes or until the grains are tender (all the water should have gone). Serve hot with *dal makhani* (see page 18) and *boondi raita* (see page 69).

This wholewheat bread is flavoured with ajowan and baked in a *tandoor*. Ajowan is a close relative of parsley and the seeds have a sharp, thyme-like aroma. It is used in northern India in particular, especially in the Punjab. Known to temper the effects of a legume-based diet, by relieving wind and indigestion, ajowan is used in the preparation of savoury foods, such as snacks, pastries, vegetable dishes, and breads. Use it in moderation, because a small amount gives a strong flavour.

khasta roti
खस्ता रोटी
oven-baked wholewheat bread

makes about 10 pancakes

500g (1lb 2oz) wholewheat flour,
  plus extra for dusting

2tsp caster sugar

¼ tsp salt

1tbsp ajowan seeds

Sieve the flour into a bowl and mix with the sugar, salt, ajowan seeds and 300ml (10½fl oz) cold water. Knead for 10 minutes into a firm dough. Cover with a damp cloth and set aside in a warm place for 15 minutes. Preheat the oven to 180°C/350°F/ gas mark 4. Divide the dough into 10 equal balls. Dust with flour and roll out into 10cm (4 inch) circles. Prick evenly with a fork, place on a baking tray and bake for 8–10 minutes until light brown in colour and slightly bubbly on the surface. Serve with *galouti kababs* (see page 50) or *murgh seekh kababs* (see page 39).

Breakfast in the north wouldn't be complete without a couple of *aloo parathas* to start the day. Many northerners eat the plainer variety minus the potato stuffing, simply called *parathas*. They can be stuffed with any kind of vegetable filling, such as cauliflower, carrots, peas, and even radishes. The *parathas* tend to be served with a dollop of home-made white butter (*makhan*).

aloo parathas
आलु पराठा
potato-stuffed unleavened breads

makes 8 *parathas*

400g (14oz) white or red potatoes, peeled, boiled and coarsely mashed

2 green finger chillies, finely chopped

½ tsp salt

pinch of ajowan seeds (optional)

large knob of butter or *ghee*, plus extra for buttering

300g (10½oz) wholewheat flour, plus extra for dusting

1tbsp vegetable oil

In a bowl, mix the mashed potatoes, chillies, salt, ajowan seeds, if using, and knob of butter. Pour the flour into a second bowl, then, with your hands, knead it with 155ml (5½fl oz) tepid water for 5–7 minutes to make a pliable dough. Divide the dough into 8 equal balls and cover them with a damp cloth while you work. Slightly flatten one ball to make a small bowl shape. In the centre of the "bowl" place 1tbsp potato mixture. Bring the edges of the dough together to cover the filling and flatten again. Dust a smooth surface with flour and roll out each disc, with the join down, into a circle 15cm (6 inches) in diameter.

Heat a griddle pan over a medium to high heat and grease with oil. Smear butter over one side of each *paratha* and place this side on to the heated pan. As this side is cooking (which should take about a minute until it is slightly bubbled on the surface with light brown spots), butter the other side, then turn the *paratha* over and cook for a minute. Wrap in foil while you cook the rest. Lower the heat for the following *parathas*. Serve with a *raita* (see page 69) or pickle.

Wholewheat flours are usually used for making *chapatis, parathas, naans,* and all kinds of unleavened and leavened flatbreads. However, Indians' love of "western" white bread has resulted in nationwide experimentation that's leaving its mark on various products. Chilli bread is just one of them.

masala pav
मसाला पाव
chilli bread

225g (8oz) plain flour, sifted
¼ tsp salt
20g (¾oz) butter
1 small Spanish onion, very finely
  chopped

½ tsp hot chilli powder
1 green finger chilli, finely chopped
few sprigs of coriander leaves, chopped
1tsp dried yeast
1tsp granulated sugar

Put the flour in a large bowl and mix with the salt, butter, onion, chilli powder, green chilli, and coriander leaves. In a small bowl, mix the yeast with the sugar and 1tsp tepid water. When it froths, mix the yeast with the flour mixture and add 75–100ml (2½–3½fl oz) warm water to make a pliable dough. Knead for 6 minutes, then cover with a damp cloth and leave to rise for 1 hour.

Preheat the oven to 220°C/425°F/gas mark 7. Place the dough into a greased, small loaf tin and place in the very hot oven for 25 minutes until light brown and well risen. Slice and serve hot with a cup of tea or at lunch, smeared with *dhania ki chatni* (see page 72) and served with *tamatar shorba* (see page 26) or *masala murgh shorba* (see page 44). The bread should keep for 3 days in the refrigerator. It's also good as hot buttered toast.

Phulkas are usually made and served around the time the meal is eaten. They are cooked fresh practically every day in almost every household in northern India. The Hindi term *"hulka phulka"* means light and fluffy. The longer you knead the dough for, the lighter and more delicate the *phulkas*.

phulka

फुलका
puffed unleavened bread

makes 5–6 *phulkas*

200g (7oz) wholewheat flour, plus a little extra for dusting
1tsp vegetable oil
butter or *ghee*, to serve

Sift the flour into a bowl and add the oil. Stir in enough tepid water to make a soft dough – approximately 130ml (4½fl oz). Knead for 10 minutes. The dough should not be sticky. Break off golf-ball size pieces of dough and roll out on a floured surface into circles about 15cm (6 inches) in diameter. As you roll, dust the *chapati* with a little flour, which prevents it from sticking and allows the rolling pin to move freely.

Heat a heavy-based frying pan over a medium heat. Place a circle of dough in the pan and cook for 20 seconds on one side, turn over and wait until bubbles rise to the surface. Turn over again and allow the other side to cook; with the back of a tablespoon press firmly around the edges so the *chapati* puffs up. Repeat with the other *chapatis*. Serve immediately with a little butter or *ghee* or just plain. Traditionally *phulkas* are eaten with *aloo phalia* (see page 20), *aloo gobhi* (see page 30), *laal maas* (see page 47), and *shahi paneer* (see page 21).

Garam masala literally means a mixture of hot spices. As the name suggests it does bring heat to a recipe. It's an integral part of most curry dishes in northern India, acting as a seasoning. Made by blending dry roasted spices such as cumin, black pepper, cardamoms and cinnamon into a powder, only a small amount is used, usually at the end of cooking, to add a subtle flavour. Many variations are available depending on the region and personal taste. Though various blends can be bought, many Indian households prepare their own.

garam masala
गरम मसाला
hot spice mix

1tsp whole cloves
3–4 bay leaves
2 green cardamoms, seeds only
4 black cardamoms, seeds only
1tsp caraway seeds (optional)
12 black peppercorns
½ tsp freshly grated nutmeg

Heat a pan and add all the ingredients excluding the nutmeg. Stir for 30 seconds to release the aromas. Remove from the heat, add the nutmeg, then grind the mixture in a coffee mill, or with a pestle and mortar, to a fine powder. Store in an airtight container away from sunlight for up to 6 months. Use at the end of cooking, sprinkling sparingly.

The process of peeling and chopping ginger and crushing garlic can become slightly tedious, which is why many Indian households prepare this mixture in advance. So, when a recipe requests ginger and garlic, the ready-prepared blend can be whipped out and added to taste. A recipe for 4 people needs approximately 2tsp.

adrak lahsun ka masala
अदरक लहसुन का मसाल
ginger and garlic paste

makes approx 100ml (3½fl oz)
115g (4oz) root ginger, peeled and coarsely chopped
115g (4oz) garlic cloves

In a food processor blend the ginger and garlic together to a smooth paste. If necessary, add 15ml (1tsbp) cold water. Store in a covered container in the refrigerator for up to 2 weeks.

murgh ka saalan
मुर्ग का सालन
chicken stock

makes approx 500ml (18fl oz)
680g (1½lb) chicken pieces with bones
4 cloves
4 black peppercorns
2.5cm (1 inch) cinnamon stick
2 garlic cloves cloves

Place the chicken pieces in a heavy-based pan with 1 litre (1¾ pints) cold water. Add the cloves, peppercorns, cinnamon, and garlic. Bring to the boil, cover and simmer for 30 minutes. Strain the stock. Let it cool, cover and refrigerate for up to a week. The stock can be frozen in small plastic containers for up to 3 months.

Boondis are pearl drops of chickpea flour deep-fried in oil. They are readily available from any Asian store or can be obtained by mail order or online.

boondi raita

बूंदी रायता

yogurt and chickpea flour salad

Serves 4

115g (4oz) *boondi*

200ml (7fl oz) natural unsweetened yogurt

¼ tsp ground cumin

1tsp caster sugar

¼ tsp salt

2 green finger chillies, finely chopped

20g (¾oz) coriander leaves, roughly chopped

Soak the *boondis* in a bowl of boiling hot water for about 5 minutes to soften and to remove some of the oil. Drain and rinse with cold water. Whisk 100ml (3½fl oz) cold water with the yogurt, then mix in the cumin, sugar, salt, green chillies, and coriander leaves. Add the *boondis* and mix well. Chill for at least 20 minutes. *Boondi raita* can be stored in an airtight container in the refrigerator for up to 3 days. Serve as a side salad with *jeera chawal* (see page 56).

Yogurt, or curd as it is known in India, is a staple throughout the regions. It is eaten plain or in *raitas* or hot chutneys with vegetables and fruit added; it is beaten thin with water and seasoned as a summer drink; it is added by the spoonful and browned in gravies. This cool yogurt salad is the perfect antidote to hot spicy dishes, or as an accompaniment to a lentil and vegetable dish such as *dal makhani* (see page 18) or *aloo phalia* (see page 20).

tadka raita
तड्का रायता
seasoned yogurt

serves 2–3

255ml (9fl oz) natural unsweetened yogurt

1 small Spanish onion, finely sliced

1 medium tomato, finely chopped

1 green finger chilli, finely chopped

¼ tsp salt

1tbsp vegetable oil

¼ tsp brown or black mustard seeds

4 curry leaves

10 unsalted peanuts (optional), skinned

In a bowl, whip the yogurt until it is creamy. Fold in the onion, tomato, green chilli, and salt. Heat the oil in a small frying pan, then add the mustard seeds and curry leaves. Fry for a few seconds, then tip in the peanuts, if using. Fry for a minute, making sure they don't burn. When the mixture has cooled, gently add it to the yogurt. Serve chilled.

In India, salads used to be classed as food for people on strict diets or the sick. Because western food has become increasingly popular, and lifestyles more frantic, salads are now part of many Indian meals. This dressing can be used on any salad leaves or served simply on its own as a relish or a dip.

dahi dip
दही डिप
yogurt-based dressing

serves 4

½ large cucumber, coarsely grated

1 medium onion, coarsely chopped

100ml (3½fl oz) natural unsweetened
  yogurt

1tsp freshly ground black pepper

coriander leaves, roughly chopped

1tbsp lemon juice

¼tsp salt

1tsp ground cumin

Purée all the ingredients in a blender until fairly smooth. Serve chilled, or pour on to the salad just before serving.

Coriander chutney is an eternal favourite: it goes well with many snacks, such as *pakoras* (see page 32). It is often used as a relish when making vegetable sandwiches in India.

dhania ki chatni
धनिया की चटनी
coriander chutney

serves 6

100g (3¾oz) coriander leaves, roughly chopped
3 green finger chillies, roughly chopped
1 garlic clove, roughly chopped (optional)
½ tsp salt
1tsp lemon juice
1tsp demerara sugar

Place all the ingredients in a blender and blitz until the mixture becomes a coarse paste: add 4–5tbsp cold water to ease blending. Alternatively, use a pestle and mortar. This chutney can be stored in an airtight, non-metallic container for up to 4 days in the refrigerator.

Chutneys bring out the flavours of any Indian meal, and they are also used to stimulate the taste buds. There are two kinds of Indian chutneys: cooked and fresh uncooked. The uncooked ones are usually made with fruit, but they are sometimes prepared with vegetables. However, whether fresh or cooked, all chutneys are sweet and spicy. Most kinds of apple make good chutney, but I've opted for the tartness of the cooking varieties for this one.

seb ki chatni
सेब की चटनी
apple chutney

serves 4

1 tsp salt
2 large cooking apples, peeled and cut into 1cm (⅖ inch) cubes
1 tbsp vegetable oil
½ tsp mustard powder
½ tsp turmeric
½ tsp medium-hot chilli powder
pinch of asafoetida (optional)
1 tbsp demerara sugar

Sprinkle the salt over the chopped apples. Heat the oil in a heavy-based pan. Add the mustard powder, turmeric, chilli powder and asafoetida, if using. Mix the spices together for a few seconds with a wooden spoon, then add the sugar, followed by the apples. Cook over a medium heat for 5-10 minutes. Cool and serve with the main meal. It's good with *aloo parathas* (see page 58) or *galouti kababs* (see page 50). Store in an airtight, non-metallic container in the refrigerator for up to 4 days.

The fruit of a tropical tree, tamarind is indispensable in most South and North Indian homes. Its curved, brown bean pods contain a sticky pulp with 1-10 shiny black seeds. This pulp is used for its sweet, sour, fruity taste. It is available as a fibrous, compressed slab, a bottled concentrate, or dried pods. Jaggery is dehydrated sugar cane juice that complements tamarind's sourness – its closest equivalent is demerara sugar. Tamarind chutney makes a great tangy relish that usually accompanies chickpea flour-based savoury snacks.

imli ki chatni
इमली की चटनी
tamarind chutney

serves 6
200g (7oz) tamarind block
1tbsp groundnut oil
½ tsp ground cumin
½ tsp medium-hot or hot chilli powder
½ tsp salt
50g (1¼oz) jaggery or 4tbsp demerara sugar

Steep the tamarind in 400ml (14fl oz) boiling water, breaking the pulp into pieces. Leave for 10 minutes. Sieve the tamarind to extract the pulp and juice. Discard the fibrous husk that's left behind. Heat the oil in a heavy-based pan and add the cumin, chilli powder, and salt, followed by the jaggery and tamarind. Mix well. Cook on a low heat for 5–6 minutes. Cool completely. Store the chutney in an airtight, non-metallic container for up to a week in the refrigerator. Serve with *pakoras* (see page 32) or other deep-fried snacks.

This chutney is good with deep-fried snacks such as *pakoras,* or a meal of *jeera chawal* (see page 56) and lentils.

pudina ki chatni
पुदीने की चटनी
mint chutney

serves 4

50g (1¼oz) mint leaves

1 medium Spanish onion, roughly chopped

2 green finger chillies, roughly chopped

1tbsp lemon juice

½ tsp salt

30g (1oz) coriander leaves, roughly chopped

1tsp demerara sugar

Place all the ingredients in a blender with 3–4tbsp water and blend to a thick paste. Store in an airtight, non-metallic container in the refrigerator for up to 4 days. Add 1tbsp natural yogurt to make mint *raita.*

Most Indians use garlic in every aspect of their cooking. It is one of the ingredients that forms the base of most curries, tempered or seasoned in oil to release its aroma. This recipe uses garlic in its raw form. This gives the chutney a strong and sharp flavour that is neutralized by adding yogurt to the mixture. Make sure the garlic is fresh by checking that the bulb feels firm and the cloves are held tightly together.

lahsun ki chatni
लहसुन की चटनी
garlic chutney

serves 4

6 plump garlic cloves, coarsely chopped

1tsp ground cumin

1tsp medium-hot or hot chilli powder

2tbsp natural unsweetened yogurt

½ tsp salt

Blend all the ingredients together into a thick smooth paste. Serve with *phulkas* (see page 62) and *dal makhani* (see page 18) or *aloo gobhi* (see page 30). It goes well with *murgh tangri kababs* (see page 37).

Fig trees are grown in the plains of Central India. Being very sweet, figs are usually eaten in their natural state. Very ripe figs are sun-dried and used to make sweets as well as chutneys. Legend has it that chutney comes from the Hindu word *"chatni"*, meaning savouring, or relishing, or pleasing to the palate. Indians make chutneys out of almost anything, including meat, fish, and poultry. But this fig chutney is sweet and savoury.

anjeer ki chatni
अंजीर की चटनी
fig chutney

serves 4

2tbsp vegetable oil

1 small Spanish onion, finely chopped

2 garlic cloves, roughly chopped

500g (1lb 2oz) dried figs, roughly chopped

1tbsp caster sugar

4 green finger chillies, roughly chopped

4tbsp malt vinegar

4tbsp white vinegar

Heat the oil in a small frying pan. Fry the onion and garlic in the oil until golden brown. Set aside. Place the remaining ingredients in a blender with the fried onions and garlic and whiz to a smooth, thick paste. Chill for at least 30 minutes before serving. The chutney can be stored in an airtight, non-metallic container in the refrigerator for up to 1 month. Serve with *murgh seekh kababs* (see page 39) or *Kakori kababs* (see page 48) as a dip.

Lemon or lime pickle is ubiquitous throughout India. Pickles are mainly made during the summer with vegetables and fruits such as mango, lime, and green chillies. They are a spicy and delightful addition to a meal, though their strong flavours can make them an acquired taste. There are innumerable recipes for this pickle, but my mother's method is one of the simplest: it contains only one spice and no oil. The lemons are pickled and preserved in their own juice. Ajowan seeds resemble thyme in flavour and are used in making onion *bhajis*.

nimbu ka achaar
नींबू का आचार
sweet lemon pickle

serves 20
12 unwaxed medium lemons
155g (5½oz) salt
300g (10½oz) granulated sugar
1tsp *garam masala*
1tbsp ajowan seeds

Wash the lemons and soak in cold water for 30 minutes. Dry, then top and tail them. Cut each one into 8 pieces by cutting them in half and then each half into 4 pieces. Mix all the ingredients together in a bowl. Pour into a non-metallic, airtight jar and keep in a warm place, such as a cupboard, for a week. Every so often give the jar a shake to make sure the liquid covers all the pieces. When the lemons begin to turn dark, the pickle is ready to eat. The pickle can be stored for up to 8 months. Serve as a relish with any Indian dish, such as *parathas* (see page 58) or *phulkas* (see page 62) with *aloo gobhi* (see page 30) or *ghia ki sabzi* (see page 29).

Gaajar-ka-halwa is an all-time favourite northern Indian pudding. The basic *halva* recipe uses clarified butter or *ghee* with sugar and semolina. However, the use of vegetables such as potatoes, beetroots, marrows, and carrots in Indian *halvas* is quite common. *Gaajar-ka-halwa* can be served warm or chilled.

gaajar ka halwa
गाजर का हलवा
cardamom-flavoured carrot dessert

serves 2

3 green cardamoms

1tsp unsalted butter or *ghee*

200g (7oz) carrots, peeled and finely grated

300ml (10½fl oz) full-fat milk

2tbsp demerara sugar

12 blanched almonds, coarsely chopped

20g (¾oz) sultanas

a few saffron strands, soaked in 1tbsp warm milk (optional)

Discard the outer cases of the cardamoms and crush the seeds in a pestle and mortar.

Melt the butter or *ghee* in a heavy-based pan. Add the carrots and stir over a gentle heat for a couple of minutes. Pour in the milk and cook over a medium heat for 15 minutes or until the mixture becomes thicker than double cream, and slightly firm. Stir occasionally to prevent the carrots sticking to the pan. Stir in the sugar, half the almonds, the cardamom seeds, and sultanas. Spoon into a serving bowl. If using, pour the saffron-laced milk over the pudding. Garnish with the remaining chopped almonds and serve.

Shahi tukra is a fried bread pudding from the northern region of Lucknow. It is made with slices of buttered bread, which are griddled and then soaked in creamy milk, sugar, and saffron. I've omitted the sugar here. A dish from the days of the Moguls, it needs no baking and no eggs.

shahi tukra
शाही टुकड़ा
fried bread pudding

serves 4

500ml (18fl oz) full-fat milk

150g (5¼oz) condensed milk

a few saffron strands

10–12 roasted, unsalted pistachio nuts, roughly chopped

2 green cardamoms, seeds only, crushed (optional)

30g (1oz) unsalted butter, softened

4 slices white bread

In a heavy-based pan bring the milk to the boil. Add the condensed milk followed by the saffron. Simmer the milk on a low flame for 10 minutes until it begins to thicken. Stir in the pistachio nuts and cardamoms, if using, and cook for 2 minutes. Set aside to cool.

Preheat a griddle. Spread butter on both sides of the slices of bread and cook on the griddle until they turn crispy, taking care not to brown them too much. Place them in a deep-sided dish, covering the base and then layer as necessary. Pour the milk over the bread. Leave the pudding to cool, then refrigerate for 2 hours.

Indians are said to have a sweet tooth, and an amazing collection of sweets or *mithai* (as they are called in Hindi) available to satisfy it. *Barfi* is made from milk that has been cooked slowly and reduced to a fudge-like consistency. It is then flavoured with saffron, vanilla essence, cocoa, or rose water, and nuts and fruit are often added. Eaten and served in bite-size pieces, *barfi* is treated as a dessert. Hindus traditionally welcome the five days of Diwali celebrations with sweet, sticky treats such as *habshi barfi*, which is also eaten during the winter.

habshi barfi
हब्शी बर्फी
nut fudge

serves 2–3
200g (7oz) condensed milk
2tsp unsalted butter
2tbsp full-fat milk
2 green cardamoms, seeds only, crushed (optional)

50g (1¾oz) unsalted mixed almonds, pistachios, and walnuts, coarsely crushed

In a pan, stir the condensed milk over a low-to-medium heat for a minute. Add the butter and then the milk. Continue stirring and add the cardamoms, if using. The mixture will begin to thicken and reduce; it should take around 6 minutes to become as thick as mayonnaise. Stir in the nuts – it will look like crunchy peanut butter – and heat for another minute. Place the sticky mixture on to greaseproof paper and pat into a 10cm (4 inch) square, 2cm (⅘ inch) thick. Leave to cool. Slice into 2.5cm (1 inch) squares and serve with tea.

Phirni is a smooth and creamy Punjabi dessert. It's a chilled rice flour pudding laced with cardamom. On special occasions, such as Diwali, rose water and saffron are often added.

phirni

ground rice pudding

serves 4

1tbsp unsalted almonds, cut into slivers
1tbsp unsalted pistachios, roughly chopped
750ml (26fl oz) full-fat milk
2½tbsp rice flour
5tbsp caster sugar
1tsp rose water (optional)
5 green cardamoms, seeds only, crushed
a few saffron strands (optional)

Mix the almonds and pistachios together in a small bowl. Gently heat the milk in a heavy-based pan. When it begins to boil, add the rice flour and sugar and mix well. Cook over a low heat, stirring frequently, for 2 minutes to dissolve all the sugar. Add half the chopped nuts to the milk with the rose water, if using. Continue cooking and occasionally stirring until the mixture becomes very thick. Spoon into 4 small ramekins or cups, sprinkle over the remaining nuts and leave to cool. Refrigerate for at least 1 hour. Serve chilled, garnished with the cardamom seeds and saffron strands, if using.

Lassi is the milkshake of India. Made with cold yogurt and tempered with either sweet or salty ingredients, it is drunk mainly in northern India during the hot summer months. This recipe is a spicy version of a *lassi* that is often drunk after a meal to aid digestion.

namkeen lassi

salty lassi

serves 2–3
450ml (16fl oz) natural unsweetened yogurt
1tsp ground cumin
¼ tsp salt
pinch of freshly ground black pepper (optional)
mint sprig

Blend the first 4 ingredients with 900ml (32fl oz) cold water. Serve chilled with a sprig of mint.

Rose water and *kewra* are common ingredients in Indian desserts. *Kewra* flowers have a sweet, perfumed aroma that is similar to roses, but fruitier. Only small quantities of either are needed to flavour any dessert.

mitthi lassi
sweet lassi

serves 2
1 green cardamom
100ml (3½fl oz) natural unsweetened yogurt
1½ tsp caster or demerara sugar
1tsp rose water or *kewra*
4 mint leaves, coarsely chopped

Remove the seeds from the cardamom and discard the outer case. Blitz all the ingredients except the mint with 200ml (7fl oz) cold water in a blender. Serve chilled decorated with mint.

This variation on the basic *lassi* recipe is made using a fruit that is synonymous with India. I've used ready-made mango pulp for extra sweetness, but a fresh pulped large or medium mango can be substituted.

aam ka lassi
आम की लस्सी
mango lassi

serves 2
100ml (3½fl oz) single cream
200ml (7fl oz) full-fat milk
400ml (14fl oz) natural unsweetened yogurt
400ml (14fl oz) mango pulp
4tsp caster sugar

Blend the ingredients together and serve with ice.

Lassi flavourings include vanilla, rose water, mint, cumin, black pepper, cardamom, or even green chillies. Other ingredients can be added, such as nuts and fruit.

vanilla lassi
वनीला लस्सी
vanilla lassi

serves 2–3
100ml (3½fl oz) single cream
200ml (7fl oz) full-fat milk
400ml (14fl oz) natural unsweetened yogurt
¼tsp vanilla essence
4tsp caster sugar
freshly grated nutmeg, to serve (optional)
mint sprig (optional)

Whisk the first 5 ingredients together and serve chilled. Garnish with freshly grated nutmeg or a sprig of mint, if using.

"Thandai" literally means "a cooler". It is a sweetly spiced northern Indian milkshake which is drunk during the colourful Hindu festival of Holi, celebrating the arrival of spring. In North India, temperatures in summer can reach 40°C, and stay there for some months. During this time *thandai* may be laced with a drug called *bhaang*, which produces a feeling of euphoria and intoxication.

thandai
ठडाई
syrup drink

makes approx 100ml (3½fl oz) syrup

4tbsp caster sugar

pinch of saffron (optional)

10 black peppercorns

3–4 green cardamoms, seeds only, or ½ tsp cardamom powder

10 unsalted cashew nuts

10 blanched almonds

2tsp fennel seeds or ground fennel

4tsp rose water

Gently heat the sugar in a small saucepan with 2tbsp water until it dissolves into a syrup, stirring occasionally. Turn off the heat. In a coffee mill or pestle and mortar, grind all the dry ingredients to a fine powder. Add to the sugar syrup with the rose water and mix. Strain the mixture through a tea strainer; it should yield approximately 100ml (3½fl oz) syrup. Store the syrup in an airtight container and refrigerate for up to 4 days.

Add 2tsp *thandai* syrup to 200–255ml (7–9fl oz) cold milk and mix thoroughly.

Nimbu pani is an Indian version of lemonade, and you can make either sweet or salty versions.

nimbu pani
नींबू पानी
lemon ginger soda

serves 2–3

3cm (1⅕inches) root ginger, peeled and finely grated

80g (2¾oz) caster sugar

juice of 2 lemons

2 cloves

2 black peppercorns

pinch of ground cumin

mint sprig

Place all the ingredients except the mint in a heavy-based saucepan with 450ml (16fl oz) cold water. Heat gently to dissolve the sugar, stirring occasionally, before simmering for 50 minutes. Strain the mixture and cool. Place in the refrigerator to chill. Serve with ice and garnished with a sprig of mint.

The South is home to some of India's hottest and most exotic dishes, for hot food helps to cool the body, and the region experiences very high temperatures. Fresh or green spices – often ground with water, lime juice, fresh coconut or vinegar to make wet paste spice mixtures – are used in abundance. The South boasts a rich and varied cuisine, and there are many Hindu communities who practice vegetarianism, as well as Muslims and Christians who enjoy non-vegetarian food.

The South Indian meal is traditionally served on a banana leaf. Each dish has its own place on the leaf and is served in a set order, with rice. Indeed, rice is the region's staple and is one of the main ingredients in several South Indian fast foods and snacks, such as *dosa* (pancakes), *idli* (steamed rice cakes) and *vada* (fried savoury doughnuts or fritters), which are all made of fermented rice and lentils and are now popular throughout India. *Dosas* are cooked on an oiled griddle, and there are several

south
दक्षिण

variations. The basic batter is made from rice and dehusked split skinned black lentils, which have been soaked overnight and ground wet into a creamy batter. These pancakes, from the states of Tamil Nadu and Karnataka, are paper-thin and crispy. Various fillings, sweet or savoury, are prepared for them, and stuffed *dosas* are called *masala dosas*.

The chutneys that accompany *dosas* and other South Indian meals are made from peanuts, tamarind, coconut, lentils, fresh coriander, and red and green chillies, and most of these chutneys, as well as pickles and relishes, are very hot.

Southern Indians tend to cook in oil rather than *ghee* (clarified butter). The food is less greasy than in the North, with many dishes being boiled or steamed. Coconut oil is commonly used, and the wide availability of coconut has influenced the region's culinary creations. Tamarind is the region's most popular souring agent, and curry leaves are used in most savoury dishes as a flavouring or garnish. South Indian lentil and curry preparations are more watery and soupier than their North Indian counterparts. Being a coastal area, the South also specializes in seafood.

Hyderabad, the capital of Andhra Pradesh, was the seat of the wealthy *nizams* or kings who ruled the capital for around 500 years. Today, the region is home to a unique non-vegetarian cuisine, which is similar to Mogul cooking: *ghee* is used more often than in the rest of the South, spices are added to cream and butter, dishes are garnished with almonds, pistachio nuts, cashew nuts, and raisins, while meats are cooked in rice. These rice dishes are known as *biryanis,* and are renowned throughout India. They are made with meat marinated in yogurt and spices – the rice is placed on top of the meat and is cooked on a slow flame in a clay *haandi* (vessel) sealed with dough. The flavour of the marinated meat seeps into the rice and, once the seal is broken, the aromas are released. There are simple Hyderabadi dishes such as *kitchdi* (rice and lentils) and more complex ones such as *lukmi* (deep-fried pastry dough squares stuffed with minced meat).

Kerala is a land of coconut palms, green paddy fields, and forests; a state of backwaters, lagoons, lakes and rivers where fishermen bring their catch in from the sea. It is also a land of spices such as cardamom, cinnamon, ginger, pepper, and turmeric. Chillies, fresh curry leaves, mustard seeds, tamarind and asafoetida are all essential ingredients used to create the region's hot-and-sour flavours.

Kerala has a well-developed vegetarian cuisine, but also boasts plenty of meat, poultry and seafood dishes. The food is mildly flavoured and shows gentle influences from the Portuguese, Dutch, French and English; from Hindus, Christians and Muslims.

A favourite Keralan breakfast dish is *puttu*, a rice flour dough layered with grated coconut and steamed in hollow bamboo cylinders. *Appam* is a pancake made of rice flour fermented with a little *toddy* (fermented sap of the coconut palm), and is eaten with a spicy chicken or vegetable stew.

A typical Kerala feast is referred to as a *"sadya"*. It is spread out on a clean green banana leaf, and the food is eaten with the fingers. Even the dessert, *payasam* (which tastes like rice pudding), is served on the same leafy plate. All the dishes are vegetarian and they are served in a specific order.

On the east coast running along the Bay of Bengal, Chennai (which used to be called Madras) is the capital of the state of Tamil Nadu. Here locals flavour their meat and seafood dishes with red chillies, black peppercorns and fresh curry leaves to give a strong and vibrant curry aroma. Most food consists of grains, lentils and vegetables, and particularly notable is a dish known as *pongal* (a mixture of rice and lentils boiled together and seasoned with clarified butter, cashew nuts, pepper, and cumin), served during the festival of Pongal. Tamil Nadu is also famous for its filter coffee, the making of which is almost a ritual.

Karnataka, whose capital is Bangalore, boasts a varied cuisine. India's best cardamoms and black pepper are produced here. Local vegetables are used for a wide variety of dishes, and dishes with gravy are accompanied by *kozhi roti* (dry broken pieces of *dosa*) or the soft handkerchief-like *neer dosa*. No Karnataka meal is complete without *saaru* (a clear pepper broth).

Avial is a thick, mixed vegetable dish in which the vegetables are chopped and parboiled, flavoured with yogurt, and then cooked in coconut milk (you can use any combination of vegetables). The *avial* also forms part of a vegetarian feast in Kerala known as the "*sadya*". The method of serving a *sadya* is very precise. Only after all 11 or so dishes – pickles, stews, lentils, and other delicately spiced curries and rice – are placed on a banana leaf does the person begin eating.

avial
अवियल
vegetables in coconut

serves 4

500g (1lb 2oz) mixed vegetables
(courgettes, green bananas, sprouts
cut into 2.5cm/1 inch pieces; peeled
potatoes cut into 1.25cm/½ inch
cubes; sliced carrots and aubergines;
and trimmed green beans)
pinch of turmeric

1½ tsp ground cumin
4 green finger chillies, chopped
125g (4½oz) grated fresh coconut
1 medium Spanish onion, chopped
½ tsp salt
1tbsp natural unsweetened yogurt
¼ tsp tamarind concentrate
8–10 curry leaves

Place all the vegetables in a heavy-based pan. Add 255ml (9fl oz) boiling water
and the turmeric and simmer for 5–10 minutes or until tender.

Meanwhile, grind the cumin, green chillies, 100g (3½oz) coconut, the onion, and
salt together in a pestle and mortar, or blender, with about 6tbsp cold water to
make a coarse paste. Add the paste and yogurt to the cooked vegetables and stir.
Lower the heat and simmer for 2 minutes. Stir in the tamarind and simmer for
4 minutes more. Garnish with the curry leaves and remaining desiccated
coconut and serve hot with *parottas* (see page 131).

A *thoran* is a fried, gravy-less dish of finely chopped meat or seafood or of vegetables. It is marinated with a mixture of coconut, chillies, mild spices, onions, and mustard seeds. The mustard seeds give *thorans* a pleasantly sharp flavour.

cheera thoran
चीरा थोरान
chilli spinach

serves 2–3

255g (9oz) fresh spinach leaves, stems removed

1tbsp groundnut or vegetable oil

½tsp brown or black mustard seeds

1 medium dried red chilli

3–4 curry leaves

1 small Spanish onion, roughly chopped

¼tsp salt

1 garlic clove, roughly chopped

1 green finger chilli, roughly chopped

1tbsp desiccated coconut

Wash the spinach thoroughly to remove any mud. Heat the oil in a heavy-based pan. Add the mustard seeds. When they splutter, add the red chilli and curry leaves, followed by half the onion, the salt, and spinach. Cook over a medium heat for 3 minutes to wilt the spinach, stirring frequently. In a blender or pestle and mortar, blitz the garlic, green chilli, coconut, and the remaining onion into a coarse paste. Add to the spinach. Cook for 3 minutes over a low heat. Serve hot with *basmati chawal* (see page 54), *kozhi Kundapuri* (see page 122), and *eliya mulakarachathu* (see page 116).

The most basic of Indian dishes is probably *dal*. It is found in every region accompanying curry or rice and *chapatis*. *Sambar* is a soupy lentil dish, made with a spice mixture called *sambar podi* (*masala*), which is eaten throughout southern India. *Sambar* is usually fiery hot and consists of red chillies, pepper, turmeric, coriander seeds, fenugreek, and cumin, with a few skinned split black lentils. It is served with rice, *dosas* (rice and lentil pancakes), *idlis* (steamed rice cakes) or *vadas* (deep-fried, fermented rice and lentil cakes).

sambar

south indian lentils and vegetables

serves 4

4tbsp *tuvar dal* or *arhar dal*

¼ tsp turmeric

1½ tbsp sunflower or vegetable oil

1 medium carrot, peeled and thinly sliced

115g (4oz) white or red potatoes, peeled and cut into 2cm (⅘ inch) cubes

50g (1¾oz) green beans, topped and tailed

1 medium tomato, chopped

1½ tsp *sambar podi* (see page 134)

¼ tsp salt

¼ tsp tamarind concentrate

pinch of asafoetida

1 medium dried red chilli

5–6 curry leaves

¼ tsp cumin seeds

Pick over the lentils (*dal*) to check for small stones, then wash under cold running water. In a heavy-based pan, boil the lentils with the turmeric, 1tsp of the oil, and 255ml (9fl oz) cold water for 30 minutes. Add the vegetables, tomato, and *sambar podi* with 255ml (9fl oz) boiling water, cover and simmer for 10 minutes. Add the salt and tamarind concentrate and continue simmering for 3 minutes.

In a small frying pan, heat the remaining oil and tip in the asafoetida, chilli, curry leaves, and cumin seeds. When they sizzle, tip this oily mixture into the pan of lentils. Mix well. Serve hot with *basmati chawal* (see page 54) and *dosay ka masala* (see page 106) with *thengai chatnil* (see page 140).

Dosa is a popular South Indian pancake that is made from a fermented batter of rice and skinned split black lentils. The rice and lentils are soaked separately in water overnight, then blended and combined. The mixture then ferments for another 10 hours. This bubbly batter is used to make thin and crispy pancakes, which are filled with all kinds of stuffings. One of the most popular fillings is this spicy potato mixture. It's a great dish, which can be served without the *dosas*.

dosay ka masala

मसाला डोसा फिलिंग

masala dosa filling

serves 2–3

1tsp skinned split black lentils or *urad dal*

2tbsp vegetable oil

pinch of asafoetida

1tsp cumin seeds

½ tsp brown or black mustard seeds

8–10 curry leaves

3 medium dried red chillies, stalks removed

½ tsp turmeric

1 medium Spanish onion, finely sliced

¼ tsp salt

1tsp peeled and finely grated root ginger

600g (1lb 5oz) white or red potatoes, peeled, diced and boiled

1 medium tomato, roughly chopped

20g (¾oz) coriander leaves, finely chopped

Pick over the lentils for small stones. Soak the lentils in a cup of hot water for 5 minutes. Heat the oil in a frying pan. Add the asafoetida, then the cumin and mustard seeds. When they splutter, add the curry leaves, lentils, red chillies, turmeric, and onion, and mix. Fry over a medium heat for 4 minutes, then add the salt, ginger, potatoes, tomato, and coriander leaves and mix well. Serve hot with *elemicha sadam* (see page 130) and *thengai chatnil* (see page 140).

Tapioca is an important product of the American plant cassava, but the main producers are now in Asia and Africa. Tapioca is usually used for making milk puddings in the West, but in South India it is found in various savoury preparations, such as these spicy patties of tapioca pearls and potato.

sabudana aloo vada
साबूदाना आलू
tapioca and potato patties

makes 15–20 patties

200g (7oz) tapioca
400g (14oz) white potatoes, peeled and boiled
2 green finger chillies, finely chopped
½ tsp salt
12 whole peanuts, roasted and crushed (optional)
vegetable or groundnut oil
30g (1oz) coriander leaves, roughly chopped

Soak the tapioca in about 255ml (9fl oz) cold water for about 10 minutes. It should swell and absorb all the water. Coarsely mash the potatoes, chillies, salt, peanuts, if using, and coriander together. Mix in the tapioca. Heat the oil in a fryer or wok to 180°C/350°F. To check that the oil is hot enough, drop a small piece of the potato mixture into the oil: if it sizzles, the oil is ready. With wet hands, roll the potato mixture into spheres the size of a golf ball, then flatten the balls to make patties. Depending on the size of the fryer, place a few patties at a time in the oil. Fry on one side for 2 minutes, then turn them over and fry for another 2 minutes until golden brown. Remove with a slotted spoon and drain them on a kitchen paper. Serve hot with *mulagu chatni* (see page 138) or *thengai chatnil* (see page 140).

Okra in Hindi is known as *bhindi*. It's a vegetable that is prepared throughout India. When cut, okra releases a sticky substance that has thickening properties, but adding yogurt prevents the okra from sticking together. When selecting okra, opt for small-to-medium pods that are firm, crisp, and bright in colour. The pods should snap cleanly when broken. Cooked okra can be stored in the refrigerator for up to 4 days.

vendekkai pachadi
वेनडाका किचीडी
okra in yogurt

serves 2–3

200g (7oz) okra

3tbsp vegetable or groundnut oil

¼ tsp brown or black mustard seeds

¼ tsp fenugreek seeds (optional)

8–10 curry leaves

2 medium dried red chillies, stalks removed

1 medium Spanish onion, finely sliced

¼ tsp turmeric

¼ tsp salt

2tbsp natural unsweetened yogurt

Wash the okra and dry thoroughly. Cut off the stalks. Slice the pods into 2cm (⅘ inch) rounds. Heat the oil in a heavy-based pan and sprinkle in the mustard seeds, fenugreek, if using, curry leaves, and chillies. When the seeds start to crackle, add the onion and sauté for a minute. Stir in the turmeric and salt. Add the okra and fry well, stirring occasionally, over a medium heat for 8 minutes. Stir in the yogurt and simmer gently for 2 minutes. Serve hot with *parottas* (see page 131), *sambar* (see page 105) or *kozhi Kerala curry* (see page 121), and *elemicha sadam* (see page 130).

South Indian food is largely non-greasy, roasted, and steamed. Rice is the staple grain and forms the basis of every meal. It is often served with *sambar* (see page 105), dry and curried vegetables, a curd or yogurt dish called *pachadi* (see page 136), and this lentil soup. *Rasam* is similar to *sambar*, which is a thicker version with vegetables. *Rasam* can be served on its own.

rasam
रसम
thin lentil soup

serves 2

4tbsp *tuvar dal* **or** *arhar dal*

pinch of turmeric

4tsp vegetable oil

¼ tsp salt

¼ tsp black or brown mustard seeds

pinch of asafoetida

5–6 curry leaves

¼ tsp cumin seeds

1 green finger chilli

¼ tsp tamarind concentrate

Pick over the lentils (*dal*) to check for small stones. Rinse under cold running water. In a heavy-based pan, bring the lentils to the boil in 400ml (14fl oz) water, the turmeric and 1tsp of the oil. Cover and simmer for 30 minutes or until the lentils are cooked. Add 200ml (7fl oz) boiling water to the lentils and mix in the salt. Heat the remaining oil in a separate pan. Add the mustard seeds, asafoetida, curry leaves, cumin seeds, green chilli, and tamarind concentrate and mix well. When the seeds splutter, remove from the heat and add the lentils with their liquid. Returnn to the heat, stir and cook for a minute. Serve in a mug.

Chinese fishing nets are used in Fort Cochin to haul shrimps and prawns, among other fish, from the sea. Prawns are popular in the South and partner the ubiquitous coconut very well, inspiring many recipes, which also use the pungent spices that the Malabar Coast in Kerala is famous for, such as cardamom, pepper, cinnamon, cloves, and nutmeg.

thenga kuda eraal
तेंगा ऊडान इराळ
prawns with coconut

serves 4

½ tsp tamarind concentrate

½ tsp hot chilli powder

1 tsp ground cumin

½ tsp turmeric

¼ tsp salt

1 tbsp groundnut or vegetable oil

1 garlic clove, sliced

12 king prawns, cooked, shelled, and deveined

½ tsp peeled and finely grated root ginger

1 green finger chilli, finely chopped (optional)

100ml (3½fl oz) coconut cream

2 tbsp roughly chopped coriander leaves

In a bowl, mix 2tbsp cold water, the tamarind, chilli powder, cumin, turmeric, and salt. Heat the oil in a heavy-based pan over a medium heat. Add the garlic and prawns. Sauté for 2 minutes. Stir in the ginger, green chilli, if using, and tamarind mixture. Add 100ml (3½fl oz) boiling water and simmer for 2 minutes. Carefully add the coconut cream because it tends to spit. Simmer for 3 minutes, then stir in the coriander leaves. Serve immediately with *basmati chawal* (see page 54), *sambar* (see page 105), *thengai chatnil* (see page 140), and *parottas* (see page 131).

This is a traditional fish curry from Kerala. It is cooked in an earthenware vessel known as a *chatti* which adds to the flavour. It is usually made with coconut oil, but I have used groundnut oil. I have also reduced the amount of chilli powder considerably. South Indian curries tend to be extremely hot, and as the climate gets hotter the further south you travel, so does the food.

eliya mulakarachathu
एलिया मुल्करचत्तू
kerala fish curry

serves 2–3

½ tsp hot chilli powder

5–6 shallots or 1 small Spanish onion, finely chopped

½ tsp turmeric

2 garlic cloves, roughly chopped

2 tsp peeled and finely grated root ginger

¼ tsp salt

2 tbsp groundnut oil

5–6 curry leaves

¼ tsp fenugreek seeds

pinch of brown or black mustard seeds

½ tsp tamarind concentrate

500g (1lb 2oz) whole mackerel, scaled and gutted

Place the chilli powder, shallots or onion, half the turmeric, the garlic, ginger, and salt in a blender and blitz to a fairly fine paste. Alternatively, use a pestle and mortar. Heat the oil in a large frying pan and add the curry leaves, fenugreek, and mustard seeds. When the seeds have popped, add the spicy paste and gently cook over a low heat for 4 minutes. In a small bowl, mix the tamarind with 4 tbsp cold water, then add to the pan and stir.

Wash the mackerel and pat dry with kitchen paper. Cut 3-4 diagonal slits on each side of the fish and season with the remaining turmeric. Carefully add the fish to the pan, nose to tail, cover and simmer for 10 minutes on a low heat or until the sauce thickens and the fish is cooked. For extra sauce, stir in 3 tbsp boiling water and simmer briefly. Serve hot with *basmati chawal* (see page 54).

Kerala is a state of backwaters, lagoons, lakes, and rivers where fishermen bring in shrimp, prawns, lobsters, mussels, squid, sea bass, catfish, kingfish and seerfish. They net a quarter of India's total fish catch. People of all religions – Jews, Muslims, Christians, Buddhists, Jains – and castes live side by side and have adapted their food habits to create a unique cuisine using the local produce. *Meen molee* is fish stewed in coconut milk. It is usually prepared with seerfish, but haddock or cod are just as good.

meen molee

मीन मोली

fish curry cooked in coconut

serves 2–3

3 garlic cloves

2 green finger chillies

5cm square of root ginger, peeled

3tbsp groundnut oil

1 small Spanish onion, finely sliced

5–6 curry leaves (optional)

¼tsp turmeric

¼tsp salt

200ml (7fl oz) coconut milk

500g (1lb 2oz) haddock fillets, cut into 4cm (1⅗ inch) wide pieces

2 medium tomatoes, coarsely chopped

Mince the garlic, chillies, and ginger together in a food processor. Heat the oil in a fryer or wok and fry the onion with the curry leaves, if using, for 4 minutes over a medium heat or until the onion looks glazed. Stir in the minced garlic mixture with the turmeric and salt. Fry for 2 minutes. Add 100ml (3½fl oz) coconut milk with 155ml (5½fl oz) boiling water. Simmer for 2 minutes and then add the fish pieces and gently simmer for 5–6 minutes. Add half the tomato and the remaining coconut milk and simmer for 3–4 minutes more. Garnish with the remaining chopped tomato. Serve hot with *parottas* (see page 131) or *basmati chawal* (see page 54).

Spicy fish delicacies, rice-based dishes, and a wide variety of fruit are perennial favourites on the Mangalorean menu. They also love *kozhi roti*, a dry, crisp, almost wafer-thin rice pancake filled with chicken curry as a spicy treat. Often the *rotis* are bought from a local store and a *kozhi*, or chicken curry, like this one is prepared at home.

mangalorean kozhi
कोरी मेंगलौर
mangalorean chicken

serves 3

4tbsp vegetable oil

4tbsp natural unsweetened yogurt

1½tsp coarsely ground black pepper

2 garlic cloves, crushed

1tsp peeled and finely grated root ginger

1tsp ground cumin

¼tsp ground cinnamon

¼tsp salt

1tsp lemon juice

500g (1lb 2oz) boneless and skinless chicken breast, cut into 4cm (2⅗ inch) cubes

1 medium onion, finely chopped

½tsp turmeric

In a bowl, mix together 1tbsp of the oil, the yogurt, black pepper, garlic, ginger, cumin, cinnamon, salt, and lemon juice. Add the chicken, cover and refrigerate for half an hour to marinate. Heat the remaining oil in a heavy-based pan. Add the onion and turmeric. Gently fry for 5 minutes to soften the onion. Add the chicken pieces with any marinade. Fry over a medium heat for 5 minutes until the chicken is golden brown all over, then add 100ml (3½fl oz) boiling water and simmer for 10 minutes or until the chicken is thoroughly cooked. Add more water if you like more sauce. Top with a generous grinding of black pepper. Serve hot with *basmati chawal* (see page 54), *elemicha sadam* (see page 130) or *parottas* (see page 131), and *thengai chatnil* (see page 140).

Curry leaves are extensively used in southern India, less so in the North. They were introduced to Malaysia by the many South Indian (mostly Tamil) immigrants during the British colonial era. However, outside the Indian subcontinent, they are rarely found. Imported fresh leaves can be purchased in the West, but if you can't find any, the dried variety will suffice: the flavour of curry leaves is so distinctive. Rumour has it that the word "curry" came from the Indian name for these leaves which is *"kari patta"*.

kerala kozhi estew
केरला कोरी करी
kerala chicken curry

serves 4

4 green finger chillies, roughly chopped

½ tsp turmeric

¼ tsp ground coriander

¼ tsp ground cinnamon

1 tsp peeled and finely grated root ginger

4 garlic cloves, roughly chopped

¼ tsp salt

4 tbsp groundnut oil

5–6 curry leaves

2–4 cloves

1 large Spanish onion, finely sliced

1kg (2lb 3oz) chicken drumsticks and thighs, skinned and pricked

200ml (7fl oz) coconut milk

2 green finger chillies, slit lengthways

In a blender, or with a pestle and mortar, blitz the chillies, turmeric, coriander, cinnamon, ginger, garlic, and salt with 1tbsp of the oil and 2tbsp cold water to make a coarse paste. Heat the remaining oil in a heavy-based pan. Add the curry leaves, cloves, and onion and fry over a medium heat for 3 minutes. Add the paste and fry for a minute. Tip in the chicken pieces and fry for 10 minutes on a medium to low heat. Rinse out the blender or mortar that contained the paste with 200ml (7fl oz) cold water. Mix this with the coconut milk. Pour over the chicken and mix well. Cover the pan and simmer for 15 minutes, or until the chicken is cooked. Garnish with green chillies and serve hot with *elemicha sadam* (see page 130) and *cheera thoran* (see page 104).

Chicken is called *kozhi* in the Kundapur region of southern India, where the meat is usually cooked with coconut and spices. Kundapur is on the coastal belt of the Arabian Sea, in the state of Karnataka: it's also known as the "town of the sun". The Kundapuris swear by this simple but flavourful dish.

kozhi kundapuri
कोरी कुंडापुरी
south indian style chicken

serves 4

30g (1oz) butter or *ghee*

2tbsp groundnut or sunflower oil

2 medium Spanish onions, chunkily chopped

1kg (2lb 3oz) chicken drumsticks and thighs, with bones, skinless

¼tsp salt

1tsp hot chilli powder

1tsp *garam masala*

155ml (5½fl oz) coconut milk

1tbsp lemon juice

a few sprigs coriander, roughly chopped

Melt the butter or *ghee* in a heavy-based pan with the oil. Tip in the onions. Fry over a medium heat for 6–7 minutes or until lightly fried. Add the chicken and salt and fry for 6 minutes to brown all over. Cover and cook on a low heat for 18 minutes or until the chicken is thoroughly cooked. Stir in the chilli powder and *garam masala* and cook, uncovered, for a further 3 minutes, stirring frequently. Add 155ml (5½fl oz) boiling water, the coconut milk, and lemon juice. Simmer for 3 minutes. Garnish with coriander leaves. Serve hot with parottas (see page 131), *elemicha sadam* (see page 130), *vendekkai pachadi* (see page 110), and *thengai chatnil* (see page 140).

Chettinad is a town in Chennai, formerly known as Madras, where most of the curries are hot but deliciously flavoured with whole and ground spices. I've reduced the amount of chilli in this recipe – it's customary to use 1tsp hot chilli powder per person.

kozhi chettinad
चेतीनाड कोरी करी
chettinad chicken

serves 2–3

2tbsp vegetable oil
¼tsp brown mustard seeds
pinch of asafoetida
5–6 curry leaves, roughly chopped
400g (14oz) chicken fillets, skinned and cut into 2.5cm (1 inch) cubes
1tsp ground cumin
½tsp ground coriander
¼tsp turmeric
¼tsp salt
¼tsp hot chilli powder
2tbsp coconut cream
juice of ½ lime
1tsp peeled and finely grated root ginger
30g (1oz) coriander leaves, roughly chopped

Heat the oil in a heavy-based pan or wok over a medium heat. To check that it has reached the right temperature, sprinkle in a few of the mustard seeds: if they pop, it is hot enough and you can add the remainder. Add the asafoetida and curry leaves and fry for 30 seconds, stirring continuously, until everything is well combined and aromatic. Tip in the chicken cubes and fry for 5 minutes over a medium heat or until golden brown. Add the cumin, coriander, turmeric, salt, and chilli powder and cook for 2 minutes, stirring continuously.

In a bowl, mix 4tbsp boiling water with the coconut and add to the chicken. Stir for a minute, then add the lime juice. Mix thoroughly, simmer for 3–4 minutes, then add the ginger and simmer for another minute or until the chicken is cooked. Garnish with coriander leaves and serve hot with *chawal basmati* (see page 54) or *parottas* (see page 131), *dosay ka masala* (see page 106), and *avial* (see page 102).

Keralan cuisine has been influenced by many traditions. It's a creative combination of vegetables, meat, and seafood, with a variety of spices, almost always cooked in coconut milk, and is mildly flavoured. The Keralans have adopted colonial British stew recipes, adding spices to make them their own. In southern India, stew is made with coconut milk and Malabar Coast spices. In Kerala in particular it is often eaten with *appams* (rice flour pancakes) for breakfast. The Keralans use small pieces of chicken on the bone but I tend to use boneless pieces.

kozhi kerala
केरल कोरी स्टु
kerala chicken stew

serves 3–4

4tbsp groundnut oil

1 medium Spanish onion, sliced

2 green finger chillies, finely chopped

1tsp peeled and coarsely grated root ginger

2 garlic cloves, crushed

¼tsp hot chilli powder

1tsp ground coriander

½tsp turmeric

½tsp salt

500g (1lb 2oz) skinless chicken breasts, cut into 2.5cm (1 inch) pieces

2 medium tomatoes, roughly chopped

300g (10½oz) white potatoes, peeled and cut into 4cm (1⅗inch) cubes

330ml (11½fl oz) coconut milk

6–8 curry leaves (optional)

4 shallots, finely sliced (optional)

pinch of *garam masala*

Heat 3tbsp of the oil in a pan and sauté the onion and chillies for 3 minutes. Stir in the ginger, garlic, chilli powder, coriander, turmeric, and salt. Add the chicken and fry on a low-to-medium heat for 8 minutes, until the chicken is lightly browned. Tip in the tomatoes and potatoes and cook for 2 minutes. Pour in 100ml (3½fl oz) of the coconut milk and simmer for 6 minutes. Add the remaining coconut milk with 200ml (7fl oz) boiling water. Simmer for 10 minutes, until the potatoes are tender and the chicken is cooked. In a separate pan, heat the remaining oil and add the curry leaves and shallots, if using. Fry for 5 minutes until golden brown. Sprinkle the *garam masala* over the stew and swirl in an extra 2tbsp coconut milk. Serve hot garnished with the fried shallots and curry leaves.

The cuisine of Hyderabad, the capital city of Andhra Pradesh, ranges from the Hyderabadi style, with its strong Islamic influence, to a pure Andhra hot and spicy style. The cooking of Hyderabad is rich and aromatic and uses many exotic spices, as well as *ghee*, nuts, dried fruit and lamb. Hyderabad is also famous for its *biryanis* – rice dishes flavoured with meat or vegetables.

hyderabadi biryani
हैदराबादी बिरयानी
lamb rice

serves 4

500g (1lb 2oz) stewing lamb, cut into bite-size chunks

2tsp *adrak lahsun ka masala* **(see page 66)**

2.5cm (1 inch) cinnamon stick

2 cloves

4 green cardamoms, seeds only

½ –1tsp medium-hot chilli powder

1tbsp natural unsweetened yogurt

1tbsp lemon juice

6tbsp groundnut oil

½tsp salt

1 medium Spanish onion, finely sliced

200g (7oz) white basmati rice, or any other long-grain rice

4tbsp full-fat or semi-skimmed milk

a few saffron strands

15g (½oz) butter or *ghee*

Mix the lamb with the *adrak lahsun ka masala*, cinnamon, cloves, cardamoms, chilli, yogurt, lemon juice, 1tbsp of the oil and the salt. Cover and refrigerate for 30–45 minutes. Heat 3tbsp of the oil in a small frying pan, and fry the onion for 5 minutes or until crisp and golden brown. Set aside. Rinse the rice thoroughly in cold running water and place in a pan with 400ml (14fl oz) boiling water. Cover and boil for 8 minutes or until the rice is half cooked. The grains should be soft on the outside but still hard in the centre. Gently warm the milk and soak the saffron strands for a few minutes.

Preheat the oven to 180°C/350°F/gas mark 4. Heat the remaining oil in a heavy-based pan and fry the marinated meat for 15 minutes until well browned. Stir in the fried onion. Grease the base of a large heavy-based casserole with the butter or *ghee*. Add the meat mixture followed by the parboiled rice. Pack the rice firmly into the casserole. Pour the saffron-laced milk over the rice. Cover tightly and bake for 45–50 minutes. Serve hot with *raita* and *pudina ki chatni* (see page 77). It's good with extra fried onions, sultanas, and roasted cashew nuts, too.

Coconut trees provide life and sustenance in southern India. Kerala's climate is ideal for coconut farming: the leaves are used for roofing; the central stem of the leaves makes firewood; the trunk is used for building timber; the coir in the husk is woven for matting; the shell of the nut is used as a drinking cup and even to serve food. And, of course, the coconut flesh is an excellent food.

thengai rice
थेंगा राइस
coconut rice

serves 2–3

1tbsp groundnut or vegetable oil

400g (14oz) freshly cooked white basmati rice

¼tsp brown or black mustard seeds

pinch of asafoetida

6 whole unsalted cashew nuts

4–5 curry leaves

1 medium dried red chilli

1tsp skinned split black lentils or *urad dal* (optional)

¼tsp salt

50g (1¾oz) freshly grated or desiccated coconut

few sprigs of coriander, roughly chopped

Heat the oil in a pan large enough to hold the cooked rice. Throw in the mustard seeds, asafoetida, cashew nuts, curry leaves, chilli, black lentils, and salt. Stir over a medium heat for a minute. Add the coconut and fry for another minute. Add the cooked rice and gently mix. Heat through. Sprinkle with coriander. Serve either on its own or as an accompaniment to a lentil dish or curry, such as *sambar* (see page 105) and *kozhi Chettinad* (see page 123), with *vendekkai pachadi* (see page 110).

Basmati rice is an authentic Indian long-grained rice that has a unique nutty flavour. It is very popular in India and all over the world and is used in a wide variety of rice dishes: plain steamed rice, *pulaos*, *pilafs*, *biryanis* or just different types of fried rice. Special occasion rice dishes are usually made with basmati rice.

elemicha sadam
एलामिचा सादम
lemon rice

serves 2–3

200g (7oz) white basmati rice
1tsp skinned split black lentils or *urad dal*
1tbsp groundnut or vegetable oil
½ tsp brown or black mustard seeds
2 medium dried red chillies
5–6 curry leaves
¼ tsp salt
¼ tsp turmeric
1tbsp lemon juice

Wash the rice in a colander or sieve under cold running water for at least 30 seconds. Pick over the lentils to check for small stones. Heat the oil in a heavy-based pan. Add the mustard seeds. When they pop and crackle, add the lentils, red chillies, curry leaves, salt, and turmeric and stir for a few seconds. Add the rice and mix well, then pour in 500ml (18fl oz) boiling water. Cover tightly and simmer for 5 minutes. Add the lemon juice. Replace the lid and simmer for 8 minutes more (all the water should be absorbed). Serve hot with *sambar* (see page 105), *kozhi Kerala* (see page 121) and *vendekkai pachadi* (see page 110).

Though South Indians love rice, *parottas* are eaten instead as part of their evening meal because rice is considered too heavy for that time of day. A *parotta* is a griddled, unleavened bread similar to the North's *parathas* (see page 58).

parottas
पराठा
unleavened yogurt breads

makes 6 *parottas*
200g (7oz) plain flour, sifted
45g (1½oz) butter
2tbsp natural unsweetened yogurt
5tbsp full-fat milk
2½tbsp sunflower or vegetable oil

Mix together the flour, 15g (½oz) of the butter, the yogurt, milk, and 1tsp of the oil. Knead for 8 minutes into a soft, pliable dough. Cover with a damp cloth and set aside in a warm place for 15 minutes.

Heat a griddle or frying pan, and grease with 1tsp of the oil. Divide the dough into 6 equal-size balls and keep them covered with a damp cloth to prevent them drying out. Roll out a dough ball into a 10cm (4 inch) circle. Smear 1 tsp of the butter on one side and roll up the disc. Fold the roll shape into a neat little bundle and then twist it a couple of times. Roll out the dough again into a 15cm (6 inch) disc. Repeat with the other dough balls. Place a disc onto the hot griddle and cook each side for 2 minutes. Grease the griddle again with 1tsp oil before cooking each *parotta*. Serve immediately with *kozhi kerala* (see page 121) and *thyru pachadi* (see page 136).

Sambar is a lentil dish prepared daily in almost every South Indian household. It's an accompaniment to many dishes, including the steamed rice cakes known as *idlis* and savoury pancakes or *dosas*, and is usually served with rice alongside a curry. The basis for a good *sambar* is the mixture of spices or *sambar masala*. The powder provides a smooth velvet-like thickening to a finished sauce and it is regularly prepared fresh, but it can be made in advance. Use 1½ tsp for a recipe that serves 4 people.

sambar podi
साम्बर पोडी
mixed spice powder

makes 4 tbsp

2tsp skinned split black lentils or *urad dal*

1tsp cumin seeds

2tsp coriander seeds

1tsp fenugreek seeds

1tsp brown or black mustard seeds

6 medium red chillies

4 fresh black peppercorns

2tsp turmeric

¼ tsp asafoetida (optional)

Heat a frying pan, then dry roast the black lentils, cumin seeds, coriander seeds, fenugreek seeds, mustard seeds, red chillies, and peppercorns for a minute to release the aromas of the whole spices. Cool for a couple of minutes. Add the turmeric and asafoetida, if using, and grind to a smooth powder in a coffee mill or with a pestle and mortar. Store in an airtight container in a cool, dark place for up to 6 months.

Pachadis are salads made with whole spices, more often than not, yogurt and sometimes coconut. The *pachadi* is South India's answer to the North Indian *raita*. A *pachadi* accompanies the main meal and is one of the dishes that makes up the *sadya* – the Keralan vegetarian platter.

thyru pachadi
थ्योरू पचडि
spicy yogurt salad

serves 2–3

4tbsp vegetable or sunflower oil

4 shallots, finely chopped

6 green finger chillies, sliced

2tsp peeled and finely grated root
  ginger

½tsp brown or black mustard seeds

5–6 curry leaves

pinch of fenugreek seeds (optional)

2 medium dried red chillies, broken
  in half, stalks removed

255ml (9fl oz) natural unsweetened
  yogurt, whisked until thick

¼tsp salt

small handful of coriander leaves,
  finely chopped

Heat 3tbsp oil in a frying pan over a medium heat for 5 minutes. Sauté the shallots until golden, remove from the oil and set aside. Fry the green chillies and ginger in the pan for 2 minutes and remove. Add the remaining oil to the pan with the mustard, curry leaves, fenugreek, if using, and red chillies. Gently fry for 1 minute. Pour in the yogurt, lower the flame and keep stirring for a minute. Add the salt, fried shallots, green chillies and ginger, and cook for a few seconds. Do not boil. Leave to cool. Garnish with coriander and serve chilled with *elemicha sadam* (see page 130). For extra flavour, mix 1tbsp freshly grated coconut with 1tsp freshly grated ginger, 4–5 finely chopped shallots, and a pinch of cumin seeds, and blitz to a fine paste in a blender. Stir this into the yogurt before it is added to the pan.

This is another variety of yogurt salad, seasoned with chilli and cumin, which can be served with *avial* (see page 102) or a lentil curry and rice.

vellarikka pachadi
वेलारिक्का पचडी
cucumber yogurt salad

serves 4
155ml (5½fl oz) natural unsweetened
  yogurt
½ tsp ground cumin
1 tbsp finely chopped coriander leaves
¼ tsp salt

1 medium cucumber, roughly grated
1 tsp sunflower oil
2 green finger chillies, slit
  lengthways
1 tbsp unsalted peanuts, crushed
  (optional)

Whisk the yogurt until it is smooth and thick. Mix in the cumin, coriander leaves, and salt. Squeeze out as much water as you can from the grated cucumber and fold into the yogurt.

Heat the oil in a small frying pan. Add the chillies and peanuts. Fry for a minute, then set aside to cool for a couple of minutes. Mix well with the yogurt. Chill for at least 30 minutes before serving.

Chillies are available in many forms: fresh, dried, powdered, and flaked. Most Indians use all kinds of chilli peppers, depending on the dish. South Indians use a dried form of a red chilli that is extremely hot. Dried chillies are often fried in hot oil to release their fire power, or soaked in water to soften them ready for easy blending.

mulagu chatni
मूलागु चटनी
red chilli chutney

serves 6

**10 medium dried red chillies,
  stalks removed**

½ tsp tamarind concentrate

2 garlic cloves, crushed

2tsp demerara sugar

¼ tsp salt

1tsp vegetable oil

Soak the chillies in boiling water for 15 minutes. Drain, reserving the water. Mix 2tbsp of this water with the tamarind, garlic, sugar, salt, and oil. Blend this with the softened chillies in a blender, or with a pestle and mortar. If you wish, fry ½tsp each of cumin and mustard seeds with 5 dried red chillies in 2tsp oil for 1 minute and add to the chutney as a garnish. Serve with any type of *kabab*.

Chutney or "*chatni*" is a Sanskrit word meaning "for licking" or savouring which is precisely its purpose at the dinner table together with the other dishes at a meal. This chutney is made with coconut, the basis for almost every recipe in coastal India. It can also be used as a sandwich spread.

thengai chatni
थेंगा चटनी
coconut chutney

serves 4

1tsp seedless tamarind pulp

100g (3¾oz) fresh coconut, grated, or desiccated coconut

½ tsp salt

2 green finger chillies

½ tsp cumin seeds

1tbsp vegetable or sunflower oil

¼ tsp brown or black mustard seeds

2 medium dried red chillies

½ tsp skinned split black lentils or *urad dal*

8–10 curry leaves

Soak the tamarind in 1tbsp warm water to extract the juice. Strain to remove the fibrous parts. Mix this juice with 1tbsp cold water, the coconut, salt, green chillies, and cumin seeds. Blitz the mixture in a blender, or with a pestle and mortar, until it becomes a rough paste. Spoon into a bowl.

Heat the oil in a small pan. Add the mustard seeds and when they pop, add the red chillies, followed by the black lentils, and curry leaves. Stir well for 30 seconds. Carefully place this seasoning on top of the coconut chutney. Store in an airtight, non-metallic container in the refrigerator for up to 3 days. This is good with *Kerala kozhi estew* (see page 121) and *dosay ka masala* (see page 106).

Malai khumani is a popular recipe that was created in the princely southern state of Hyderabad. The sweet tooth of Hyderabadis is legendary. No meal is ever complete without a sweet and this dessert is a favourite at weddings, when the fresh apricot stone's kernel is removed and used as a garnish. It can be served with cream, custard or ice-cream.

malai khumani
मलाई खुमानी
apricot nut dessert

serves 4

50g (1¾oz) caster sugar
255g (9oz) dried apricots, roughly chopped
200ml (7fl oz) double cream, stiffly whipped
2 drops rose water or vanilla essence
55g (2oz) chopped pistachios

In a heavy-based pan, gently heat the sugar in 400ml (14fl oz) cold water, stirring occasionally until all the sugar has dissolved. Add 200g (7oz) of the apricots and simmer for 12 minutes. Drain. Stir the rose water or vanilla essence into the whipped cream. Fold in the aprictors and spoon into 4 ramekins or glasses. Serve chilled garnished with the chopped pistachios and the remaining dried apricots.

When it's time to celebrate, there will always be some kind of sweet dish prepared. *Payasam* is the traditional pudding made during the festival of *Onam*. It is made from milk simmered with sugar, cashew nuts, often vermicelli or lentils, and then topped with raisins. This *payasam* is made with rice.

payasam
पायासम
sweet rice pudding

serves 6

100g (3¾oz) white basmati rice

15–20 unsalted cashew nuts, whole

30g (1oz) mixed raisins and sultanas

800ml (28½fl oz) semi-skimmed milk

200g (7oz) condensed milk

2 green cardamoms, seeds only, crushed

7–8 unsalted cashew nuts, crushed

Rinse the rice thoroughly under cold running water for at least 30 seconds. Soak the cashew nuts, raisins, and sultanas in boiling water for 5–10 minutes to soften them. In a heavy-based pan, bring 500ml (18fl oz) of the milk to the boil. Add the rice and gently simmer on a low heat for 10 minutes, stirring occasionally to prevent the rice sticking. Add 100ml (3½fl oz) more milk and the condensed milk and simmer for 10 more minutes, stirring occasionally. Mix in the drained whole cashew nuts, raisins, sultanas, and the cardamoms. Simmer for 5 minutes. Add the remaining 200ml (7fl oz) milk and continue cooking for 20 minutes, stirring frequently to prevent the rice sticking to the pan, until the rice is tender and the mixture has become quite thick. Spoon into 6 small ramekins and garnish with crushed, unsalted cashew nuts. Serve hot or chilled.

These nuts are prepared to mark the beginning of spring throughout India, but particularly in Andhra Pradesh, where Hindus make all kinds of sweets to celebrate *Ugadi* in March/April. This festival marks the new year and the day that Lord Brahma created the world.

jeedi pappu
जीडि पाप्प
sugar-coated cashew nuts

200g (7oz) unsalted cashew nuts, whole
255g (9oz) caster sugar

Preheat the oven 110°C/225°F/gas mark ¼. Place the cashew nuts on a tray and bake for 10 minutes until golden brown. Set aside to cool. Gently heat the sugar and 155ml (5½fl oz) cold water in a heavy-based pan, stirring well until all the sugar has dissolved and the mixture becomes thick and stringy. Add the cashew nuts and mix well for approximately 30 seconds. Spread the cashew nuts on to a sheet of greaseproof paper. Separate the nuts with a metal spoon while they are still warm. Leave to cool. Store the nuts in an airtight container in a cool, dark place for up to 15 days.

Across the Cochin region, roadside vendors deep-fry thousands of banana slices in large black vessels filled with coconut oil. You'll also find jackfruit, tapioca, and yam chips. Often the bananas are cut into chunks, fried, dipped in jaggery or sugar syrup, then dried and sold as sweets. This recipe is for savoury chips – with a couple of variations.

kela chips
केला चिप्स
banana chips

serves 4
500g (1lb 2oz) unripe bananas
vegetable oil, for deep-frying
¼ tsp salt
pinch of hot chilli powder (optional)

Peel the bananas with a knife or a peeler. Thinly slice each banana into 2mm (¹⁄₁₀ inch) thick rounds. Heat the oil in a fryer or a wok to 190°C/375°F. Put a banana slice in the oil. If it sizzles, the oil is hot enough. Place the banana slices, a few at a time, in the oil. Ensure that they don't stick to one another. Fry for no longer than 1½ minutes or until they are light golden. Remove with a slotted spoon and drain on kitchen paper. Sprinkle with salt and chilli powder, if using. Serve cold with drinks.

If you'd like the chips to be crunchier, soak the banana slices in salted water for 2 minutes, then drain and coat in 2tbsp rice flour before frying. Another alternative is to use ¼tsp freshly ground black pepper instead of the chilli powder.

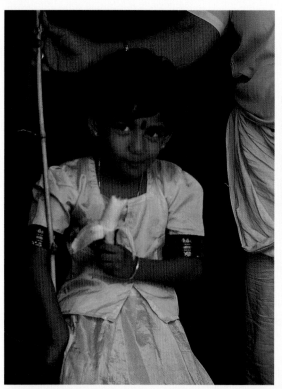

Morum vellum from Kerala is a spicy buttermilk made with curds or yogurt, grated ginger, and curry leaves. It could also be described as a fiery, hot-chilli, smoothie-style drink. It cools down the system during the hot summers but is never given as an appetizer before a meal. You're warned: it does have a kick!

morum vellum
मेरम वेल्लम
chilli and ginger buttermilk

serves 4

115ml (4fl oz) natural unsweetened yogurt

2tsp peeled and finely grated root ginger

1tbsp lemon juice

4 green finger chillies, roughly chopped

small handful of coriander leaves

1tsp ground cumin

10–12 curry leaves

pinch of asafoetida

¼ tsp salt

4 green finger chillies

Whip the yogurt until creamy. Add 255ml (9fl oz) cold water and mix well. In a blender or with a pestle and mortar, blitz the ginger, lemon juice, chopped chillies, coriander leaves, cumin, curry leaves, asafoetida, and salt into a fairly smooth paste. Blend with the yogurt. Refrigerate for 1 hour. Strain and serve chilled with crushed ice and garnished with whole green chillies.

West Bengal, and its capital city Kolkata (previously known as Calcutta), has the biggest impact on East Indian cuisine, strongly influencing the food of the surrounding states of Assam and Orissa. Bengal, the land of fish and rice, lies on the monsoon-drenched east coast of India. Its countless rivers, ponds, and lakes teem with many kinds of freshwater fish, including those that closely resemble catfish, bass, shad or mullet, and hilsa. And Bengalis prepare fish in innumerable ways: steamed or braised, stewed with greens or other vegetables, and served with sauces based on mustard or thickened with poppy seeds. You won't find these types of fish dishes anywhere else in India.

The use of mustard oil is synonymous with Bengali food. The Bengali mustard seed is pungent and dark, and gives a yellowish tinge to foods it comes into contact with. Although mustard oil is pungent when it leaves the bottle, it turns sweet when heated, and it is used both hot and cold in Bengali cooking.

east

पूरब

One speciality of Bengali cooking is the spice mix *panch phoran*, which consists of cumin seeds, onion or nigella seeds, fennel seeds, fenugreek seeds, and mustard seeds. But this is a rich and varied cuisine, influenced by the many ethnic groups who have settled in Bengal.

A Bengali meal is steeped in ritual. Traditionally, the first course is something bitter to clear the palate. Then a typical lunch or dinner will comprise of *bhaat* (rice), *dal* (lentils), *tarkari* (vegetables) and *maacher jhol* (fish curry). *Dimer jhol* (egg curry) and *mangshor jhol* (meat curry) are also favourites. Rice is served throughout, although nowadays some people prefer *roti* (griddled unleavened bread) instead. "Rainy days" mean *khichidi* (a mixture of rice, lentils, and vegetables), *begun bhaja* (fried aubergine slices), *dim bhaja* (fried eggs) and *aloo posto* (potatoes fried with poppy seeds).

On special occasions, *pulao* (basmati rice cooked in *ghee* or butter with mild spices, cashew nuts and raisins) replaces ordinary rice. A couple of fish dishes are essential on such occasions, and *chingri malai jhol* (prawns cooked in spiced coconut milk), *bhekti* (deep-fried marinated fish fillets) and *paturi* (fish steamed in banana leaves) are all popular. Then of course you need a chutney made from fruits such as tomatoes, pineapple or green mango.

Breakfast is often *luchi* (a deep-fried unleavened bread) and *tarkari* (fried or curried vegetables), although deep-fried snacks such as *shingara* (a *samosa*) are also enjoyed.

At lunchtime, office workers don't tend to sit down for a large meal, but instead they snack. They may still visit the traditional *dabba* (roadside shack), or eat from a *tiffin* (lunchbox), but the quantities they consume tend to be smaller than they used to be. Even sandwiches have become quite popular. Pavement stalls, located on street corners or near bus stands or construction sites, form the heart and soul of Kolkata's cuisine. They serve almost everything anyone might want to eat for lunch, from *maach bhaat* (fish and rice) and *tela bhajas* (fried vegetable fritters) to a *dosa* (spicy pancake) or a *kathi roll* (chicken and egg wrap). Between the pavement stalls and the five-star restaurants lies a whole universe of small, medium and large eateries in different parts of the city. Of these, the tea stalls are the first to burst into activity with their mounds of earthern *chukkars* or pots.

High tea comes with *jhaal muri* (a spicy mixture of puffed rice) – a Bengali version of western India's popular *bhelpuri*, it is laced with raw mustard oil. Western Bengal's

sweet home-made cakes have some extra charms too, and sweets are often made from cottage cheese.

When it comes to food, Assam is also impressive. The Assamese love food, although their cooking tends to be no-nonsense. As in West Bengal, fish – fried, curried with vegetables, or marinated in mustard oil and then lightly spiced – is an integral part of most meals. Bamboo shoots are used in abundance, and lemons and limes play a large part in seasoning.

The verdant land of Orissa brings vegetables and fruits that brim over with beneficial properties. Rice drawn from the emerald paddy fields finds its way to the table, sweet smelling and delicious. And there is a plentiful and diverse selection of seafood, with crabs, prawns and lobsters steeped in the ever-present rich, creamy yogurt and coconut milk. Yams, aubergines and pumpkins are also liberally cooked in yogurt, with mustard seeds giving the whole preparation that extra zing. For religious reasons, meat is rarely eaten. Mouth-watering desserts include small cakes called *pithas* (which can be savoury as well as sweet). *Chhenapodapitha*, a caramelized custard-like dessert, is also popular.

The customs, rituals and cuisine of Sikkim are as diverse as the ethnic groups that inhabit the state. Sikkimese food is an amalgam of Nepali, Tibetan and Bhutanese cooking, and is heavily influenced by Chinese cuisine. Typical Chinese soups, chow meins, chop sueys and fried rice and vegetables find their way on to everyday menus. Authentic Sikkimese food includes *momos* (steamed dumplings) stuffed with meat or vegetables and served as a starter with a clear vegetable soup, a tomato chutney, and *thupka* (a popular noodle and vegetable soup, to which meat or egg is often added).

Although Chinese food is popular throughout India, it is nowhere more evident than in the city of Kolkata. There are large Chinese communities situated near the Eastern Metropolitan Bypass Road and in the north of the city. This cosmopolitan city has it all, from the street vendors' *kathi* rolls to gourmet Indian and Chinese cuisine, but its Chinese food has a flavour all of its own.

lahsun aur hare sabzi ki noodles
लहसुन और हरे सब्जी की नूडल्स
broccoli and garlic noodles

serves 2

200g (7oz) broccoli florets, 5–6cm (2–2⅖ inch) long

2tbsp vegetable oil

1 medium Spanish onion, thinly sliced

2 garlic cloves, thinly sliced

2 green finger chillies, finely chopped

2tsp peeled and crushed root ginger

1tbsp crushed unsalted peanuts

2tbsp dark soy sauce

¼tsp salt (optional)

¼tsp coarsely ground black pepper

1tsp demerara sugar

1tsp sesame oil

200g (7oz) wheat noodles

Wash the broccoli thoroughly in cold salted water. Cook it in boiling water for 2 minutes and drain. Heat the vegetable oil in a wok or large heavy-based pan. When the oil is just smoking, add the onions and stir-fry for a minute. Tip in the garlic, chillies, and broccoli and sauté over a medium heat for 5 minutes. Stir in the ginger and peanuts. Add the soy sauce, salt, if using, black pepper, sugar, and sesame oil. Mix well.

Meanwhile, cook the noodles following the packet's instructions. Drain and quickly mix with the garlic and broccoli mixture. Serve immediately.

Deep-fried snacks, or *tela bhajas*, are the most popular street foods in East India. Vendors sell them with a bag of roasted puffed rice. Indian cheese is usually used for these cutlets, but I've used Cheddar as a variation.

aloo paneer bhaja
आलू पोनिर भाजा
potato and cheese cutlets

serves 4

300g (10½oz) white or red potatoes

100g (3¾oz) Cheddar cheese, grated

1 small Spanish onion, finely chopped

¼ tsp salt

½ tsp hot chilli powder

30g (1oz) coriander leaves, finely chopped

2tbsp plain flour, for dusting

2tbsp dried, coarse, white breadcrumbs

2tbsp cornflour

vegetable oil, for deep-frying

Peel and boil the potatoes until cooked, then drain. Mash them and mix in the cheese, onion, salt, chilli powder and coriander leaves. Dust your hands with flour and divide the potato mixture into golf ball-sized pieces. Place the breadcrumbs in a plate. Heat the oil in a fryer or wok to 180°C/350°F. Place a piece of the potato mixture in the oil; if it sizzles, the oil is ready.

In a small bowl, mix the cornflour with 1tbsp cold water to make a smooth custard-like batter. Dip each ball into the batter and then roll in the breadcrumbs so it is completely coated. Deep-fry in batches for 2–3 minutes or until the balls are golden brown.

Serve immediately with tomato ketchup or *dhania ki chatni* (see page 72) or *pudina ki chatni* (see page 77).

Like many East Indian recipes, this one is very simple, with just one spice. When buying aubergines, make sure they have a smooth surface and are light. The heavier ones contain too many seeds.

begun bhaja
बैगन भाजा
fried aubergine

serves 2

1 medium aubergine
1tsp salt
½ tsp turmeric
3tbsp mustard oil or vegetable oil
small handful of coriander leaves, roughly chopped

Remove the stems from the aubergines, then cut one lengthways in four before cutting each length in half. You should end up with eight pieces. Rub the cut surfaces with salt and turmeric and set aside for 30 minutes. Heat the oil in a frying pan and shallow-fry on a low-to-medium heat for 5 minutes on each side until golden brown. Garnish with coriander leaves.

This is the Bengali version of the celebrated *samosa* from the north of India – a small triangular pastry filled with spiced vegetables. Traditionally *shingaras* are eaten without chutney, but they are delicious with *imli ki chatni* (see page 75).

shingara
शिगारा
bengali samosa

makes approx 10 *shingaras*

300g (10½oz) wholewheat flour, plus extra for dusting

½ tsp baking powder

1½ tsp salt

600g (1lb 5oz) white or red potatoes, peeled and boiled until tender

vegetable oil, for deep-frying

½ tsp *panch phoran* or Bengali five spice mixture

½ tsp turmeric

1 tsp peeled and grated root ginger

pinch of asafoetida

4 green finger chillies, finely chopped

Sieve the flour into a bowl with the baking powder and ¼tsp of the salt. Mix well with about 155ml (5½fl oz) cold water and knead for 5–6 minutes into a smooth dough. Place the dough in a clean bowl and cover with a plate. Set aside for half an hour. Coarsely crush the potatoes. Heat 2tbsp oil in a wok and add the *panch phoran*. Once the seeds splutter, add the turmeric, ginger, remaining salt, and the asafoetida. Mix thoroughly, then add the chillies, followed by the crushed potato. Sauté for 2 minutes.

Gently heat a frying pan or a griddle. In a small bowl, mix a little flour with water to make a thick glue. Divide the dough into 10 equal balls. With the help of a dusting of flour, roll out each ball of dough into a 7.5cm (5 inch) circle. Place the circles onto the griddle for 20–30 seconds and then remove – this makes the discs easier to handle. Cut each circle in half. Taking one of the

semi-circles, apply a bit of glue to half the straight edge, then fold into a cone shape overlapping the pasted straight edge by 5mm (⅕ inch). Seal well.

Hold the cone with the pointed end downward and fill with about 1tbsp potato mixture. Seal the *shingara* with a little more glue, pressing the edges firmly together. Heat the oil for deep-frying to about 180°C/350°F. Carefully place the *shingaras*, a few at a time, into the fryer and deep-fry for 3–4 minutes until golden brown. Remove with a slotted spoon and drain on kitchen paper. Serve hot.

European cooking uses blue-grey poppy seeds, in particular for baked goods. The Indian poppy seed is smaller and off-white in colour. They are mainly used to thicken curries. *"Posto"* is the Bengali word for "poppy seeds" and they're found in countless Bengali recipes; *"aloo posto"* is the most famous.

aloo posto
आलू पोस्तो
potatoes with poppy seeds

serves 3–4

4tbsp white poppy seeds, washed

2tbsp groundnut oil

1tsp brown or black mustard seeds

400g (14oz) white potatoes, peeled, firm-boiled, and cut into 2cm (⅝ inch) cubes

1tsp ground cumin

¼tsp turmeric

¼tsp salt

1 green finger chilli, finely chopped

Soak the poppy seeds in 4tbsp hot water for 2 hours. Drain and grind them with a pestle and mortar, or in a blender, into a coarse paste. Gently heat the oil in a frying pan and add the mustard seeds. When they begin to sizzle, add the potatoes and fry for 10 minutes until they start to brown. Then add the cumin, turmeric, and salt, followed by the poppy-seed paste. Cook for 5 minutes. Mix thoroughly and then sprinkle over the green chilli. Serve with *chawal basmati* (see page 54) and a lentil dish, such as *chholar dal* (see page 164).

The cuisine of East India revolves primarily around fish, vegetables, and rice. It is lighter than North Indian food as far less cream is used in the cooking, which relies mainly on stir-frying, boiling, and steaming. This dish is a great accompaniment to a fish curry and rice.

aloo baingan jhol
आलू बैंगन झोल
potatoes and aubergine in tomato sauce

serves 2–3

2 dried medium red chillies

1tbsp coriander seeds

1tsp cumin seeds

1tsp brown or black mustard seeds

2tbsp vegetable oil

2 bay leaves (optional)

1 medium Spanish onion, thickly sliced

½ tsp turmeric

310g (11oz) white or red potatoes, peeled and cut into 2cm (⅘ inch) cubes

310g (11oz) aubergine, cut into 2.5cm (1 inch) cubes

2 garlic cloves, crushed

1 medium tomato, finely chopped

1tsp tamarind concentrate

½ tsp salt

In a coffee mill or pestle and mortar, grind the chillies, coriander, cumin, and mustard seeds to a powder. Heat the oil in a big pan and add the bay, if using, onion, and turmeric. Fry over a medium heat for 2–3 minutes. Add the potatoes and fry for a minute. Cover and cook for 7 minutes on a medium heat until the potatoes are tender. Check the potatoes don't stick halfway through cooking.

Add the aubergine and garlic and fry for a minute. Add the tomato and fry for another minute. Cover and cook for 6 minutes. Stir in the ground spices, tamarind, and salt. Add 400ml (14fl oz) boiling water. Cover and cook for 10 minutes, stirring halfway through cooking. Serve hot with *chawal basmati* (see page 54), *chholar dal* (see page 164) and *luchis* (see page 182).

Bengal *gram* is also known as *chana dal* or *gram* lentils. It is the most widely grown lentil in India. Matt yellow, with a rich nutty taste, *gram* lentils are used for making desserts, as well as being cooked with vegetables, or with meat to make *dal gosht*. *Chholar dal* is often served after a Hindu prayer ceremony and frequently contains raisins for sweetness. It may be accompanied by *luchis* (wholewheat deep-fried unleavened bread, see page 182).

chholar dal
छोलर दाल
spiced bengal gram

serves 4

155g (5½oz) Bengal *gram* or *chana dal*

¼ tsp turmeric

1 green finger chilli, slit lengthways

2 tbsp mustard oil or groundnut oil

1 bay leaf

pinch of asafoetida

2 green cardamoms, slightly crushed

⅓ inch cinnamon stick

¼ tsp nigella seeds

2 medium dried red chillies, stalks removed

1 tsp ground cumin

2 tbsp coconut cream, plus extra to garnish

¼ tsp salt

Pick over the lentils to check for stones, then place in a sieve and wash under cold running water. Soak the lentils for 2 hours in 400ml (14fl oz) cold water. Drain and place in a saucepan with 255ml (9fl oz) boiling water, the turmeric and green chilli. Simmer gently for 15–20 minutes or until the lentils are tender. Discard the green chilli and purée half the lentils in a blender. Set aside.

Heat the oil in a heavy-based pan. Add the bay leaf, asafoetida, cardamoms, cinnamon, nigella seeds, red chillies, and cumin. Stir for a minute and then carefully add the coconut cream and salt. Mix well. Tip in all the lentils, stir, and simmer for 5 minutes. Garnish with a swirl of coconut cream and serve hot.

Thupka is one of the main dishes served during the Tibetan New Year celebration, *Losar*. *"Lo"* means "year" and *"sar"* is "new". *Losar* usually falls in March. The local fare is rice and meat curry and *momos* (steamed dumplings see page 177), and, of course, *chow*, the locally made noodles. *Thupka* is a spiced consommé with a mixture of vegetables. It's also a dish that's served in many college canteens.

thupka
थुपका
vegetable noodle soup

serves 4

400g (14oz) dried medium egg
  noodles

2tbsp mustard oil or groundnut oil

1 small Spanish onion, finely
  chopped

1tsp ground cumin

¼tsp turmeric

2 garlic cloves, crushed

3tsp peeled and finely grated root
  ginger

¼tsp salt

3 green finger chillies, slit lengthways

200g (7oz) mixed vegetables, such
  as green beans, topped and tailed,
  sliced carrots, cauliflower florets

2 medium tomatoes, finely chopped

2tbsp dark soy sauce

1 litre (1¾pints) vegetable stock

½tsp ajowan seeds

¼tsp black coarsely ground pepper

200g (7oz) spinach leaves

30g (1oz) coriander leaves, coarsely
  chopped

Cook the noodles for half the manufacturer's recommended cooking time. Drain, rinse in cold water and set aside. Heat the oil in a large wok. Add the onion and fry over a medium heat until light brown. Add the cumin, turmeric, garlic, 2tsp of the ginger, salt, and chillies. Stir for a minute. Add the mixed vegetables and stir-fry for 5 minutes. Next, add the tomatoes, soy sauce, stock, ajowan, and pepper to the pan and simmer until the vegetables are tender. Add the parboiled noodles and cook over a medium heat for 3 minutes. Stir in the spinach leaves and cook for 2 more minutes. Garnish with coriander and the remaining ginger and serve hot as a starter or as a main dish with *chawal basmati* (see page 54).

Mustard oil is the main oil used in Bengali cooking. This distinguishes East Indian dishes from other Indian cuisines. Bengalis also excel in the cooking of vegetables. They prepare a variety of imaginative dishes with all sorts of vegetables, often improvising and using rejected peels, stalks, and leaves.

bhindi jhol
भींडि झोल
okra curry

serves 2
200g (7oz) okra
4tbsp mustard oil or vegetable oil
1 medium Spanish onion, thinly sliced
1tbsp *batta sharshey* **(see page 187)**
½ tsp salt

Wash the whole okra and dry thoroughly. Dry and cut into 3cm (1⅕ inch) slices and discard the stalks. Heat the oil in a wok. Add the onion and fry over a medium heat for 4 minutes. Add the okra and fry for 2 more minutes. Stir in the mustard paste and salt. Sauté for 7 minutes. Serve hot with *luchis* (see page 182).

East Indians cook many dishes with potatoes. *"Dimer"* means "egg" in Bengali and several fried-egg style dishes, such as this one, are made for breakfast. It usually has a lot of sauce, which is soaked up with *chawal basmati* (see page 54).

aloo dimer jhol
दिमेर झोल
potato and egg curry

serves 2

2 white or red potatoes, peeled and cut into 4cm (1⅗ inch) cubes

2tbsp mustard oil or groundnut oil

4 medium eggs, hard-boiled and peeled

1tsp turmeric

1 small Spanish onion, finely chopped

1 green finger chilli, finely chopped

1tsp peeled and finely grated root ginger

¼ tsp *garam masala*

½ tsp ground cumin

¼ tsp salt

sprig of coriander leaves, finely chopped (optional)

Parboil the potatoes for 10 minutes. Drain. Heat the oil in a heavy-based pan and fry the potatoes over a medium heat for 4 minutes or until golden brown. Remove them from the pan with a slotted spoon and set aside. Make 2 small slits on the eggs and fill with the turmeric. Fry the eggs for 2 minutes or until golden and remove from the pan.

Place the onion in the pan and sauté over a medium heat for 3 minutes or until golden brown. Add the chilli and ginger and fry for a minute. Add the *garam masala* and cumin and stir-fry for a minute. Add the potatoes and salt. Mix well, then pour in 200ml (7fl oz) boiling water and bring to the boil. Add the eggs and simmer for a couple of minutes until the potatoes are tender. Garnish with coriander leaves and serve hot with *chawal basmati* (see page 54) or *luchis* (see page 182).

A typical Bengali fish curry, *maacher jhol* is a light fish stew, seasoned with ground spices: ginger, cumin, coriander, chilli, and turmeric. The sauce is thin yet packed with flavour. Whole green chillies are usually added at the end of the cooking. Hoki is a succulent, white fish with a meaty texture that is perfect for this dish.

maacher jhol
माच्छेर झोल
fish curry

serves 2–3

½ tsp turmeric

1 tsp ground cumin

1 tsp ground coriander

2 green finger chillies, chopped

¼ tsp salt

30g (1oz) coriander leaves, chopped

500g (1lb 2oz) hoki or haddock fillets, skinned and cut into pieces 7.5–9cm (3–3½ inches) long

3 tbsp groundnut oil

¼ tsp cumin seeds

½ tsp brown or black mustard seeds

2 garlic cloves, crushed

1 tsp peeled and grated root ginger

1 medium Spanish onion, finely chopped

2 medium tomatoes, roughly chopped

Mix together the turmeric, ground cumin, ground coriander, chillies, salt and 20g (¾oz) coriander leaves. Coat the fish evenly with the spice mixture. Heat 2 tbsp oil in a frying pan. Fry the fish for 2 minutes on each side or until lightly browned. Drain on kitchen paper and set aside.

Heat the remaining oil in the same pan and add the cumin and mustard seeds. When they pop, add the garlic, ginger, onion, and tomatoes. Fry gently for 8 minutes. Add about 200ml (7fl oz) boiling water and stir for a minute. Return the fish to the pan and simmer for 10–12 minutes or until the sauce is brownish and not too thick and the fish is cooked. Garnish with the remaining coriander and serve hot with *chawal basmati* (see page 54) and *chholar dal* (see page 164).

With the Bay of Bengal to the east of the state of West Bengal, it is not surprising that fish is central to the region's cooking. Each morning people can be seen haggling at the open fish markets in search of the best catch of the day. They have a fondness for shellfish, too, especially prawns, which are often cooked in mildly spiced coconut milk.

chingri malai jhol
चिंगरी मलाई करी
creamy prawn curry

serves 2–3

¼ tsp salt

½ tsp turmeric

500g (1lb 2oz) peeled and cooked small prawns

1tsp peeled and roughly chopped root ginger,

2 garlic cloves, roughly chopped

1 small Spanish onion, roughly chopped

3tbsp mustard oil or groundnut oil

1 bay leaf (optional)

¼ tsp hot chilli powder

200ml (7fl oz) coconut milk

pinch of *garam masala* (optional)

pinch of mild chilli powder

Sprinkle the salt and turmeric over the prawns and set aside. Blitz the ginger, garlic, and onion into a coarse paste in a blender. Heat the oil in a large heavy-based pan or wok and tip in the prawns. Fry over a medium heat for 5 minutes. Remove the prawns with a slotted spoon and set aside. Place the bay leaf, if using, in the pan and allow it to sizzle. Add the ginger paste and fry for 6–8 minutes over a medium heat. Mix in the hot chilli powder, then stir in the fried prawns, followed by the coconut milk. Allow it to cook for a minute until piping hot – do not let it boil – then mix in the *garam masala*, if using, and remove from heat. If you like more sauce, add 200ml (7fl oz) boiling water with the coconut milk, and gently simmer for 3–4 minutes to thicken. Garnish with mild chilli powder. Serve hot with *luchis* (see page 182) and garlic and broccoli noodles (see page 156).

East Indians have added a few Chinese touches to a traditional dish to create chilli chicken. Many Indo-Chinese recipes are very Chinese, although the style of preparing them may not be authentic. Chinese-influenced dishes appear to originate in the Shantung communities from North-West China: blacksmiths and tailors who brought their particular kind of Chinese cuisine into India through Kolkata. Another explanation of the origins of Indo-Chinese food is that Indians generally love Chinese food and they've simply added more chilli, and spice.

mirch wali murgh
मिर्च वाली मुर्गी
chilli chicken

serves 2

1tbsp dark soy sauce

½tsp hot chilli powder

¼tsp salt

1tbsp cornflour

1tsp root ginger, peeled and finely grated

2 garlic cloves, finely chopped

1 tbsp malt vinegar

1tbsp tomato purée

1tsp demerara sugar

2tbsp vegetable oil or groundnut oil

1 medium Spanish onion, finely chopped

2 boneless and skinless chicken breasts, approx 310g (11oz), cut into 2cm (⅘ inch) cubes

2 green finger chillies, slit lengthways

¼tsp ground white pepper

4 spring onions, sliced

Mix together the soy sauce, chilli powder, salt, cornflour, ginger, garlic, vinegar, tomato purée, and sugar. Heat 1tbsp oil in a heavy-based pan. Fry the onion over a medium heat for 5 minutes until soft and translucent. Remove from the heat and mix the fried onions with the soy sauce paste. Add the chicken and stir to coat. Cover and leave to marinate for half an hour in the refrigerator.

Heat the pan again with the remaining oil. Add the green chillies and white pepper and fry over a low heat for a minute. Then add the marinated chicken pieces with the marinade, most of which will have been soaked up by the chicken, and fry for 10 minutes until the chicken is cooked. Garnish with spring onions and serve hot with *luchis* (see page 182) or in a *kathi* roll (see page 174) as the filling.

In Kolkata *kathi* rolls are a staple food. Pancakes, or "*parathas*", are filled with vegetables, cooked chicken or meat. Watching a *kathi* roll being made is fascinating. A ball of dough is picked up and put on to the fat on the hot *tawa* or griddle. It is flipped over and quickly spread with a beaten egg before being flipped again. Then it is taken off the *tawa* and the stuffing is added. Then the *paratha* is folded into a convenient newspaper-wrapped roll. This is a barbecued chicken roll.

kathi roll
काठी रोल
chicken and egg wrap

makes approx 6 *kathi* rolls

for the filling:

2 boneless and skinless chicken breasts, cut into 2cm (⅘ inch) cubes

1 garlic clove, crushed

1tsp peeled and grated root ginger

1tsp ground cumin

¼ tsp turmeric

pinch of *garam masala*

2 green finger chillies, finely chopped

1tsp tomato purée

1tsp lemon juice

¼ tsp salt

1tbsp vegetable oil

for the parathas:

200g (7oz) plain white flour, plus extra for dusting

¼ tsp salt

1tsp vegetable oil

100ml (3½fl oz) full-fat milk

4 medium eggs

2 red onion, thinly sliced, to serve

Mix the filling ingredients, except the oil, together. Cover and marinate for 2 hours in the fridge. Soak 6 wooden skewers in cold water. Skewer the chicken and grill, barbecue, or bake at 180°C/350°F/gas mark 4 for 20 minutes, until the chicken is cooked. Baste with oil halfway through cooking. For the *parathas*, sift the flour and salt into a large bowl. Add the oil, milk, and 1 egg and knead for 7–10 minutes. Cover with a damp cloth and leave in a warm place for 20 minutes. Divide into 6 balls and on a floured surface roll each into a 16–17cm (6½–7 inch) disc 5mm (⅖ inch) thick. Beat 3 eggs. Heat a frying pan. Put a disc on the hot pan. After a minute, turn it over. Put 1–2tbsp beaten egg on the *paratha* and spread it out. Immediately turn over the *paratha* again and cook the egged side for 30 seconds. Put some cooked chicken in the centre of each *paratha* and roll up. Serve with onion slices and *dhania ki chatni* (see page 72) mixed with yogurt.

Darjeeling is a beautiful and remote hill station in East India, with many Tibetan monasteries. *Momos* are a Tibetan-style steamed dumpling. The key to success when making the dumplings is to use white flour, and to seal completely the outer shell of each *momo*, so the filling won't dry out when they are steamed.

murgh momo
चिकन मोमो
steamed chicken dumplings

makes approx 20 *momos*

1tbsp malt vinegar

1tbsp dark soy sauce

1 small Spanish onion, finely chopped or minced

2 garlic cloves, crushed

¼ tsp salt

2 green finger chillies, finely chopped

pinch of medium-hot chilli powder

200g (7oz) boneless and skinless chicken, minced

155g (5½oz) plain white flour, plus extra for dusting

2tsp vegetable oil

Mix together the vinegar, soy, onion, garlic, salt, chillies, and chilli powder. Add the chicken and mix well. Cover and leave to marinate for 2 hours in the refrigerator. Sift the flour into a large bowl. Add 1tsp oil and mix in about 5tbsp tepid water to make a soft dough. Knead for 5–7 minutes, then cover with a damp cloth.

Divide the dough into 20 small balls. On a lightly floured surface roll out each ball as thinly as possible into a 10cm (4 inch) disc, no more than 1–2mm (¹⁄₁₀ inch) thick. Place 1tbsp chicken mixture on a disc. Fold the disc in half, making a semi-circular half-moon shape. Tightly seal the curved edges by carefully and firmly pinching the dough together. Place this *momo* on a large plate lightly dusted with flour and cover with a damp cloth while preparing the others. Lightly brush the *momos* with oil to prevent them sticking, then place in a steamer in a single layer. Steam over a high heat for 10–15 minutes, until the chicken is cooked. Serve hot with sweet chilli sauce.

This is a very rich recipe which can be made with fish, meat or vegetables, using a lot of oil and ghee. It's also highly spiced with many heat-generating ingredients, such as chilli.

murgh kalia
मुर्ग कालिया
chilli coriander chicken

serves 2

2tbsp vegetable oil

1 bay leaf (optional)

2 cloves

1 black cardamom

1 medium Spanish onion, finely chopped

1tsp peeled and finely grated root ginger

2 garlic cloves

¼tsp ground cinnamon

1tbsp butter or *ghee*

2 boneless and skinless chicken breasts, approx 310g (11oz), cut into 3cm (1⅛ inch) cubes

½tsp ground coriander

¼tsp turmeric

¼tsp salt

¼tsp hot chilli powder

1 medium tomato, finely chopped

small handful of coriander leaves, roughly chopped

Heat the oil in a pan and add the bay leaf, if using, then the cloves and cardamom. Add the onion and fry over a medium heat for 2 minutes or until it becomes translucent. Tip in the ginger, garlic, and cinnamon and fry for 2 minutes more. Add the butter or *ghee* and, when it has melted, add the chicken.

Sauté for 8–9 minutes, browning the chicken. Stir in the ground coriander, turmeric, salt, and chilli powder. Mix for a minute. Add the tomato and stir-fry for another minute. Pour in 100ml (3½fl oz) boiling water and simmer uncovered for 5 minutes until the chicken is tender. Sprinkle with coriander leaves. Serve hot with *chawal basmati (see page 54)*, *luchis (see page 182)* and *chholar dal (see page 164)*.

Most Indians have an image of Bengalis as lovers of fish and sweets. However, snacking is also taken very seriously. *Jhol khabar* is an afternoon meal consisting of light food, such as *shingaras* (Bengali *samosas,* see page 160) or *mangsher chop*, a potato patty stuffed with spiced minced lamb, coated with breadcrumbs and shallow-fried.

mangsher chop
मगशोर चौप
meat fritters

makes approx 8–10 fritters

3tbsp vegetable oil or groundnut oil

1 Spanish onion, finely chopped

2 green finger chillies, finely chopped

1tsp peeled and grated root ginger

2 garlic cloves, crushed

½tsp each salt, turmeric, ground
  cumin and ground coriander

1tsp tomato purée

450g (1lb) minced lamb

2 tsp mint leaves, finely chopped

¼tsp *garam masala*

500g (1lb 2oz) white or red
  potatoes, boiled and mashed

½tsp ground white pepper

4tbsp dried white breadcrumbs

2 medium eggs, beaten

vegetable oil, for shallow-frying

Heat the oil and fry the onion for 5 minutes. Add the chillies, ginger, and garlic and fry for 2 minutes. Add ¼tsp salt, the turmeric, cumin, and coriander and mix well. Add the tomato purée and stir in the mince and fry over a medium heat for 3 minutes to brown the meat. Add the mint and fry, stirring often, for 15 minutes or until the mince is cooked. Sprinkle over the *garam masala*. Mix the mash with ¼tsp salt and the pepper. Spread the breadcrumbs on a flat plate. Take a handful of the mash with wet hands and make a bowl shape. Place 1tbsp mince in the centre of the mash and pull the edges over it. Shape into a flat, round patty 7.5cm (3 inches) in diameter and 1.5cm (⅗ inch) thick. Repeat with the remaining mash and mince. Dip each patty in the egg, then coat evenly in breadcrumbs. Heat the oil for shallow-frying in a large frying pan. Fry in batches on each side for 2 minutes until light golden. Remove and drain on kitchen paper.

A typical Bengali lunch or dinner includes rice, lentils or *dal*, *tarkari* (fried vegetables) or vegetables, and either a *maacher jhol* (fish curry, see page 171), *dimer jhol* (egg curry, see page 169), or *mangsher jhol* (meat curry). The meat or chicken curries are usually quite rich and spicy. *Jhol* is a curry in which the sauce is not too thick.

mangshor jhol
मंगशोर झोल
meat curry

serves 2–3

300g (10½oz) stewing lamb, cut into 3–4cm (1⅕-1⅗ inch) cubes

3tbsp natural unsweetened yogurt

2tbsp mustard oil or vegetable oil

1 bay leaf (optional)

1 x 2.5cm (1 inch) cinnamon stick

2 cloves

2 green cardamom pods, bruised

1 medium Spanish onion, finely sliced

2 garlic cloves, crushed

1tsp peeled and finely grated root ginger

½tsp turmeric

½tsp hot chilli powder

1tsp ground cumin

½tsp salt

2 green finger chillies, slit lengthways

¼tsp *garam masala*

Marinate the meat in the yogurt for 20 minutes, covered, in the refrigerator. Heat the oil in a heavy-based pan. Add the bay leaf, if using, the cinnamon, cloves, and cardamoms and sauté for 30 seconds. Add the onion and garlic. Stir-fry over a medium heat for 3 minutes, then add the ginger, followed by the turmeric, chilli powder, cumin, and salt and mix well. Add the marinated meat and green chillies. Stir and cook on a low heat for 15 minutes or until the sauce has almost completely reduced. Add 400ml (14fl oz) boiling water, cover and cook on a low heat for 30 minutes until the meat is cooked through. Sprinkle over the *garam masala*. Serve hot with *chawal basmati* (see page 54).

Although Bengalis love fish and sweets, their cuisine is as varied as any other. Breakfast, for example, may be *luchis* and *tarkari* (fried vegetables). *Luchis* are small, round, unleavened puffed-up breads, made with plain flour and deep-fried. They are known as *pooris* in North India. *Luchis* or *pooris* are usually served on railway platforms with spiced potatoes or *aloo tarkari*.

luchi
थुपका
deep-fried bread

makes 15–20 *luchis*
1tbsp butter or *ghee*
200g (7oz) plain white flour
¼ tsp salt
vegetable oil, for deep-frying

Melt the butter or *ghee*. Sift the flour and salt into a bowl. Make a well in the centre and pour in the melted fat. Mix together and add approximately 130ml (4½fl oz) cold water – just enough to make a stiff dough. Knead the dough for 10 minutes, then cover it with a damp cloth.

Heat the oil in a fryer or wok to 180°C/350°F. Add a small piece of dough to the oil; if it sizzles and rises to the surface, the oil is hot enough. Take a small piece of dough the size of a squash ball and roll out on a lightly oiled surface into a 9–10cm (3½–4 inch) disc about 3mm (⅛ inch) thick. Repeat with the rest of the dough and cover with a damp cloth. Add 2 *luchis* to the oil and turn them over when they puff up – this usually takes 30 seconds – then quickly remove them when they turn light brown. Drain on kitchen paper, being careful not to squash out the air. Serve immediately with *aloo posto* (see page 162) or *aloo dimer jhol* (see page 169).

A *masala* is a mixture of spices, herbs, and other seasonings pounded together. *Masala* pastes are made with wet ingredients such as water, vinegar or yogurt. *Panch phoran* gives a distinctive flavour to pulse and vegetable dishes. It's tempered in hot oil or clarified butter before the other ingredients in a dish are added.

panch phoran
पांच फोरान
east indian five-spice mixture

makes 7tsp

1tsp fenugreek seeds

1tsp cumin seeds

1tsp fennel seeds

1tsp brown mustard seeds

1tsp nigella seeds

Mix the seeds together and store in an airtight container, in a dark place, for up to 6 months. 1tsp of whole or ground *panch phoran* can be used in a recipe to serve 4 people. To make a wet paste, mix 2tsp cold water with every 1tsp of ground *panch phoran*.

As elsewhere in India, Bengalis eat everything with their fingers. This not only helps in the business of picking out treacherous fish bones, but it also increases the awareness of texture. You can use fish pieces or a whole fish in this recipe.

maacher panch phoran
माछर पांच फोरान
five-spice fish

serves 2

400g (14oz) seabass, gutted, scaled and washed

¼ tsp salt

¼ tsp turmeric

2tbsp mustard oil

½ tsp *panch phoran*

2 green finger chillies, slit lengthways

1tbsp *batta sharshey* (page 187)

Cut several slits in the fish skin, then rub in the salt and turmeric. Heat the oil in a frying pan and fry the fish for 5 minutes, until golden, on both sides. Remove from the pan with a slotted spoon and set aside. In the same oil, fry the *panch phoran* and chillies. Stir in the *batta sharshey* and cook over a low heat for a minute. Return the fish to the pan and add 155ml (5½fl oz) boiling water. Cover and simmer for 5 minutes, until the sauce has thickened and the fish is cooked.

Mustard oil is synonymous with Bengali food. The Bengali mustard seed is dark and pungent with a sharp taste. The oil is deep yellow and gives a yellow hue to food. It is used in two forms – pungent and sweet. Brown and black mustard seeds are both used in Indian cooking. The seeds have little or no smell; the hot taste is released when they are crushed and mixed with water. Only in East India are mustard seeds made into a paste for use in marinades and curries.

batta sharshey
बाटा शोरशे
mustard paste

200g (7oz) brown mustard seeds

Grind the mustard seeds to a fine a powder with a pestle and mortar (this takes 3–4 minutes). Store the powder in an airtight container for up to 6 months. Mix with an equal volume of cold water when needed.

Chutneys add flavour to every Bengali lunch: they are incredibly versatile. *Tamatar chatni* is a good dip for savoury snacks, such as *shingaras* (see page 160) and *pakoras* (see page 32).

tamatar chatni
टमाटर चटनी
east indian tomato chutney

makes approx 310g (11oz) *chatni*

500g (1lb 2oz) medium tomatoes

1tbsp vegetable oil

¼tsp nigella seeds

¼tsp brown mustard seeds

¼tsp ground cumin

¼tsp medium-hot chilli powder

½tsp salt

100g (3¾oz) caster sugar

2tbsp liquid pectin

Immerse the tomatoes in boiling water for 2 minutes. Remove from the water, peel and discard the skin, then coarsely chop the flesh and set aside. Heat the oil in a heavy-based pan. Add the nigella and mustard seeds. When they splutter, add the cumin and chilli powder, and mix. Stir in the tomatoes and fry over a low heat for a couple of minutes. Add the salt, cover the pan and simmer for 5 minutes. Roughly mash the tomatoes. Stir in the sugar and simmer uncovered for 7 minutes. Pour in the pectin, stir well, then boil the mixture rapidly for 2 minutes until quite thick. Remove from the heat and leave to cool. Spoon the *chatni* into an airtight jar. Store in the refrigerator for up to 2 months.

Salads are usually made with cucumber, tomatoes, and onions flavoured with salt, sugar, and often a drop of lemon juice. This is the basic salad that can accompany any dish, but there are endless variations. It adds a cool, tangy crunch to any meal. And, of course, it has to contain some chilli.

pyaaz ka salaad
प्याज का सलाद
onion salad

serves 2–3

1 large Spanish or red onion, chopped
¼ tsp salt (optional)
pinch of ground black pepper
1 green finger chilli, finely chopped
2 tbsp malt vinegar

Mix all the ingredients together and serve immediately. Garnish with finely chopped coriander if you wish.

Many Bengalis choose to have sweets for lunch. As well as the sweets, or *"mishti"* as they are known, this cool yet filling sweet yogurt served in *bhars* or small earthenware pots is very popular.

mishti doi

bengali yogurt pudding

serves 2
255ml (9fl oz) full-fat milk
60g (2oz) demerara sugar
1tsp natural unsweetened yogurt
3–4 unsalted whole pistachio nuts, sliced

In a small, heavy-based pan bring the milk gently to the boil. Add 30g (1oz) of the sugar, stir to dissolve and continue boiling for 10 minutes. Remove from the heat and leave to cool slightly. Gently heat the remaining sugar in another small, heavy-based pan, stirring continuously, until it has melted and just turned brown. It will begin to look lumpy. This will take about 4 minutes. Stir 1tbsp cold water into the browning sugar. It will harden. Then tip the hardened sugar into the milk and whisk vigorously. Boil for 10 minutes, then cool to room temperature. Add the yogurt and stir well. Pour into 2 individual ramekins or a single bowl and cover. Keep in a warm, dark place, such as inside an oven or cupboard, for 2 hours until thickened. Chill in the refrigerator for 5 hours. Serve garnished with sliced pistachio nuts.

Barfi is a sweetmeat made from dried milk, which is known as *khoya*. Different ingredients are added to the *khoya* to make a variety of sweetmeats: milk *barfi* is the simplest and an everyday sweet. Other variations include adding coconut, carrots, fruit, and nuts, all of which can also be spiced with green cardamoms and saffron.

doodhi ki barfi

दूधजकीक्बरफीलवा

indian fudge

serves 4

1tsp unsalted butter

50g (1¾oz) caster sugar

155ml (5½fl oz) double cream

125g (4½oz) full-fat milk powder

Melt the butter in a heavy-based pan, then add the sugar and stir continuously over a medium heat for 3 minutes. Add the cream and simmer for 3 minutes. Add the milk powder. Continue stirring for 5 minutes or until the mixture becomes stiff and thick and it begins to leave the sides of the pan. Carefully place on to greaseproof paper and shape into a 10cm (4 inch) square about 1.5cm (⅗ inch) thick. Cool, then cut into 2cm (⅘ inch) squares and serve.

This is the definitive Indian biscuit. Countless recipes have all sorts of different ingredients but they all contain semolina and plain flour. Many decades ago, women would prepare their biscuit dough at home and take it to a communal oven or bakery for the baker to bake. The cooked biscuits would then be delivered back to them.

nan khatai
नान खताई
semolina biscuits

makes approx 16–18 biscuits

80g (2¾oz) caster sugar

80g (2¾oz) unsalted butter

3–4 drops vanilla essence

4 green cardamom pods, seeds only, crushed

155g (5½oz) plain flour, sifted

50g (1¾oz) fine semolina

Preheat the oven to 190°C/375°F/gas mark 5. Grease a baking tray. In a bowl, cream together the sugar and butter with a wooden spoon, until light and fluffy. Beat in the vanilla essence and cardamom. Add the flour and semolina. Mix into a firm paste and gently knead for 5 minutes. Dust your hands with flour. Take pieces the size of golf balls and flatten into circles about 1.5cm (⅗ inch) thick, or roll out the dough and use a biscuit cutter. Place on the baking tray at least 2.5cm (1 inch) apart and bake for 12–15 minutes or until light brown. Cool on a wire rack. Store in an airtight container for up to 3 weeks. Serve with tea made from *chai ka masala* (see page 199) and *shingaras* (see page 160).

Wherever you go in India, the one thing you can be sure of is that you'll get a cup of tea. And, as with most things, Indians like their tea spiced. *Chai ka masala* is an aromatic spiced tea created over centuries: a blend of freshly ground spices added to a boiling pot of loose-leaf tea and milk. From the big cities' railway stations to small village footpaths, there are countless *chaiwallahs* whose *chai* stalls are favourite meeting places. This spice mixture can also be used in curries.

chai ka masala
चाय का मसाला
spiced tea

3–4 x 3cm (1⅕ inch) cinnamon
  sticks or cassia bark
6 cloves
4 black peppercorns

6 green cardamoms, seeds only
1 black cardamom, seeds only
  (optional)
1tsp fennel seeds
1tsp ground ginger

Dry-roast the cinnamon or cassia bark, cloves, peppercorns, cardamoms, and fennel seeds on a griddle pan for 2 minutes. Cool. Add the ginger and grind to a fine powder with a pestle and mortar or in a coffee grinder. Cool completely and store in an airtight container, in a dark place, for up to 6 months. Add a pinch of this powder when brewing your tea: approximately ¼tsp flavours 2 cups of tea.

West India's food is hugely varied, reflecting the diverse historical influences on the region. India's third largest state, Maharashtra, blends gastronomic elements from North and South India, while its capital city Mumbai (formerly called Bombay) has evolved a cosmopolitan cuisine with international influences. Goa combines Portuguese traditions with Konkan coast cuisine, while the state of Gujarat is renowned for its sophisticated, light vegetarian meals. And the whole of West India has a popular fast-food tradition.

Maharashtra is one of India's busiest agricultural and industrial centres. Its food has light, sweet-and-sour flavours, drawn from mango, tamarind, coconut, jaggery or unrefined sugar. The dishes tend to be hot and spicy, made with chillies, fennel, fenugreek, turmeric, asafoetida, curry leaves, and green coriander.

Coconut palms cover the vast expanse of fertile land on the coastal side of Maharashtra, and alphonso, the king of mangoes, is grown in the state. Daily meals are

west परिचम

carefully planned, and usually include a green leafy vegetable, sprouted lentils, and a salad, all prepared and cooked simply.

Mumbai, once the country's commercial capital, remains the natural gateway of India, and its cosmopolitan population serves food from many different states, with seafood, and especially a flounder-like fish called pomfret, being particularly fine. Small but influential communities of Parsees, who came from Iran 1000 years ago, and other minorities such as the Sindhis, Punjabis, Goans and Khoja Muslims, have all influenced Mumbai's food. The Parsees' rich, spicy cuisine draws influences from a variety of international cooking techniques. One of their classic dishes is *dhansak* (chicken or lamb cooked with a generously spiced puréed mixture of lentils and fresh vegetables).

Mumbai's street food is exceptional. Roadside and beach shacks sell an eclectic mix of dishes, including *dosas*, pizzas, hamburgers, *pulaos*, and *biryanis*. Food is available cheaply at hawkers' joints, and if they stopped selling it much of the working population would be deprived of their favourite lunch! The most popular items include *vada pav* (*gram* flour cakes stuffed between slices of bread) and toasted sandwiches made with mint chutney and vegetables. And Mumbai's "*paan*" culture (heart-shaped betel leaf wrapped around spices and other ingredients, including pieces of the areca nut) has been raised to an art form.

Goa, sometimes known as the "pearl of the Orient", lies off the coast of the Arabian Sea. The region is blessed with some of the world's most idyllic silver-sandy beaches frilled with coconut palms. Goa became a Portuguese colony in the 16th-century, and 400 years of Portuguese rule, as well as the region's isolation from events inland, have given it a distinct identity and a cuisine to match. Arab traders and sea lords also visited or settled in the port, but the Portuguese made by far the biggest impact on the food. This is especially apparent at Christmas, when larders are filled to bursting point with rich fruit and plum cakes, biscuits and sweet or savoury pies.

Many of the fiery red concoctions that Goan cuisine is known for are Portuguese in origin. The famous *vindaloo* is from Portugal; *vinh d'alho* is garlic-flavoured wine vinegar – a Portuguese marinade. The adaptation of Portuguese food has resulted in other exotic dishes such as *sorpotel* (pork offal, including liver, kidneys, and heart, diced and cooked with chillies and tamarind) and *galinha cafreal* (fried or roasted marinated chicken).

Goa's staple food is fish, although the Christians also eat beef and pork. The region's cuisine is hot, sweet and sharp, thanks to spices such as cinnamon, cloves, and black peppercorns, and curry pastes made with coconut, red chillies, and vinegar. Coconut milk is used in abundance, and is particularly popular in fish dishes, chutneys, and desserts such as *bebinca* (a coconut layered cake).

Gujarat is home to some of India's finest vegetarian dishes. There are slight variations in eating habits and modes of preparation in its component regions: Kathiawari in the

west and Kutch in the north-west include chilli powder; south Gujaratis use fresh green chillies; and the Suratis of the south-east use far more sugar in their cooking, giving their food a sweet, tangy flavour.

Gujarat food is mainly mild. Pulses and vegetables, accompanied by breads, are popular. Dairy-based products, such as buttermilk, are also favoured, and spice pastes are made using a base of fresh root ginger and green chillies. Gujaratis enjoy sweet-and-sour flavours, and some savoury recipes use sugar, at times jaggery or unrefined sugar.

A traditional Gujarati meal is served on the silver or stainless-steel platter known as a *thali*. A *thali* meal begins with cumin-laced buttermilk, followed by hot fluffy *chapatis*, accompanied by a variety of lentils, seasonal vegetables, curds or yogurt, and pickles, then *mithais* (or sweets), and savouries (known as *farsans*), and finally rice or *kichidi* (a lentil and rice mixture). During the winter, Gujaratis make the delicious dish, *undhyoo*, using various vegetables, including potatoes, aubergines, and green beans. The Bohra community of Muslims are Gujarat's main meat eaters, and are famous for their beef dishes and hot or cold clear soups liberally mixed with cashew nuts and vegetables.

Black-eyed beans are a staple in Maharashtra and Gujarat, and are braised with spices in stews and other dishes. This is a dish which is served as part of a main meal in a *thali* or on a plate.

chawlichi bhaji
चवलीची भाजी
marathi black-eyed beans

serves 4

255g (9oz) dried black-eyed beans
2tbsp vegetable oil
¼ tsp brown or black mustard seeds
1 small white onion, finely chopped
2 green finger chillies, chopped
pinch of asafoetida (optional)
1 medium tomato, roughly chopped
½ tsp salt
handful of coriander leaves, roughly chopped

Pick over the beans to check for small stones, then place in a sieve and wash under cold running water. Soak the beans in 750ml (26fl oz) cold water for an hour. Drain and place in a saucepan with 500ml (18fl oz) cold water. Boil for 45 minutes. Drain.

Heat the oil in a heavy-based pan. Tip in the mustard seeds. When they pop, add the onion, chillies, and asafoetida, if using, and gently fry for 3 minutes. Then add the tomato, beans, and salt and fry over a medium heat for 2 minutes. Cover and simmer for 5 minutes. Sprinkle with coriander leaves and serve hot with *kaalvan* (see page 218) and *chawal basmati* (see page 54).

The aubergine originated in India, and every region will have a recipe for the "small aubergine". For this dish choose firm and smooth aubergines with shiny, unblemished skins. Aubergines can soak up a lot of oil, but this recipe requires very little oil and the aubergines are steamed.

bharleli vangi
भरलेली वांगी
stuffed aubergines

serves 4

500g (1lb 2oz) small aubergines

3tbsp vegetable oil

2 medium Spanish onions, finely chopped

2 green finger chillies, finely chopped

1tsp peeled and finely grated ginger

1tsp ground cumin

1tsp ground coriander

1tsp mango powder or *amchur*

½tsp salt

½tsp turmeric

2tbsp unsalted peanuts, crushed

30g (1oz) coriander leaves, finely chopped

Cut along almost the entire the length of each aubergine, but keeping it intact with the stalk on. Turn each aubergine by 90 degrees and make another lengthways cut, again not cutting through the stalk. Heat 2tbsp of the oil in a heavy-based pan or wok with a lid. Add the onions, chillies, and ginger and gently fry for 2 minutes or until the onion is translucent. Add the ground cumin, coriander, mango powder, salt, turmeric, and peanuts, and fry over a medium heat for a minute. Mix in the coriander leaves and remove from the heat. Using a spoon, carefully stuff the onion mixture inside each aubergine.

Heat the remaining oil in a heavy-based casserole. Place the stuffed aubergines in the pan. Cover and cook on a very low heat for 25 minutes, stirring carefully halfway through cooking. Serve hot with *chapatis* or *fodnicha bhaat* (see page 230).

Goan cuisine is a blend of influences the Goans have experienced during the centuries. The staple food is fish, among Hindus as well as Catholics. But that aside, there is a vast difference in the foods of these two communities, because Christians eat beef and pork, which are taboo in Hindu households. Christian food is heavily influenced by the Portuguese and their overseas settlements. This salad, complete with dressing, is a fine example. Lettuce is not generally available because of Goa's humid climate, so cabbage is used in abundance.

goan salada
गोअन सलादा
goanese salad

serves 4

500g (1lb 2oz) white cabbage, shredded

1 medium white onion, finely sliced

1 medium tomato, finely sliced or chopped

3 green finger chillies, finely chopped

1 tbsp malt vinegar

1½ tbsp groundnut oil

½ tsp demerara sugar

1 garlic clove, crushed

¼ tsp salt

¼ tsp crushed black peppercorns

Place the cabbage, onion, and tomato in a bowl. Mix together two-thirds of the chopped chillies, the vinegar, oil, sugar, garlic, salt, and pepper in a second bowl, and sprinkle over the vegetables just before serving. Toss the salad well. Garnish with the remaining green chillies and serve with *galinha cafreal* (see page 225) and *chawlichi bhaji* (see page 206).

These are a street food from Mumbai (Bombay), sold around beaches and in fast-food restaurants. However, my mother has always made them at home. *Batata vadas* are the West Indian version of the North's *samosas*, but they are made with chickpea flour rather than wheat flour.

batata vadas
बटाटा वड़ा
battered potato balls

makes approx 10–12 potato balls

vegetable oil, for deep-frying

½ tsp each brown mustard seeds and turmeric and ¼ tsp salt

1 tsp granulated sugar

2 green finger chillies, finely chopped

600g (1lb 5oz) white or red potatoes, peeled, boiled and coarsely chopped

30g (1oz) coriander leaves, chopped

¼ tsp each ground cumin and baking powder

150g (5¼oz) chickpea flour or *besan*

Heat 1tbsp oil in a heavy-based pan large enough to hold the potatoes. When the oil is hot, gently tip in the mustard seeds, then the turmeric, ½tsp salt, the sugar, and chillies, and mix. Add the potatoes, coarsely mashing as you mix. Add the coriander and mash to make a lumpy mixture. Remove from the heat and leave to cool.

In a bowl, mix the sifted chickpea flour with the remaining salt, the cumin and baking powder, 1tsp oil and about 130ml (4½fl oz) cold water to make a batter the consistency of runny honey. Wet your hands and roll the mash into pieces the size of golf balls. Heat the oil in a fryer or wok to 190°C/375°F. Drop a little batter into the oil: if it sizzles, the oil is hot enough. Dip a few potato balls in the batter and turn to coat them evenly. Drop the coated balls into the hot oil and fry for 4 minutes, or until the outside of the balls is a deep golden brown. Lift them out with a slotted spoon and drain on kitchen paper. Wrap in foil and keep warm while cooking all the potato balls. Serve hot with *thengai chatni* (page 140).

Gujarati cuisine is a blend of many flavours and textures, with many variations in eating habits and methods of preparation, but most Gujaratis are linked by their staunch vegetarianism. Ingredients such as yogurt, buttermilk, coconut, peanuts, sesame seeds, lime juice, and sugar are used in abundance, and dishes are often served with rice and a variety of wheat breads. *Batata nu shaak* is potatoes in a sweet-and-sour sauce.

batata nu shaak
बटाटा नू शाक
potatoes in yogurt sauce

serves 2–3

1 medium Spanish onion, roughly chopped

2 green finger chillies, roughly chopped

2tsp peeled and finely grated root ginger

2tbsp vegetable oil

pinch of asafoetida (optional)

500g (1lb 2oz) new potatoes, boiled

4–5 unsalted whole peanuts

¼tsp salt

130ml (4½fl oz) natural unsweetened yogurt

30g (1oz) coriander leaves, finely chopped

Mince the onion, chillies, and ginger together in a food processor. Heat the oil in a heavy-based pan and add the asafoetida, if using. Gently fry for a minute. Add the minced onion mixture and fry over a low heat for 6–7 minutes or until the onion is light brown. Stir in the potatoes and fry for 1 minute. Then add the peanuts and salt and mix well. Whisk the yogurt until smooth and fold into the potatoes, then simmer for a minute. Serve hot with *chawal basmati* (see page 54) and *chawlichi bhaji* (see page 206) or mixed vegetable curry.

Poha (beaten or flaked rice) is used in all kinds of savoury dishes and is the basis of this traditional Maharashtrian snack or vegetarian main dish with several variations. *Batata poha* is eaten for breakfast in some families. Quick to make, it is fairly dry, so a dollop of yogurt or chutney goes well with it. The thin variety of *poha* is used to make *chivda* (see page 215), a kind of Bombay mix.

batata poha
बटाटा पोहा
savoury rice flakes with potato

serves 3–4

2 tbsp vegetable oil

1 tsp brown or black mustard seeds

¼ tsp turmeric

1 small Spanish onion, finely chopped

200g (7oz) white potatoes, peeled and cut into 1.25cm (½ inch) cubes

2 green finger chillies, finely chopped

½ tsp salt

¼ tsp ground cumin

1 medium tomato, finely chopped

1 tsp demerara sugar (optional)

200g (7oz) rice flakes

1 tbsp lemon juice (optional)

handful of coriander leaves, roughly chopped

1 tbsp desiccated coconut

1 tbsp natural unsweetened yogurt

Heat the oil in a heavy-based pan and add the mustard seeds. When they pop, add the turmeric and mix for a few seconds. Then tip in onion, potatoes, chillies, and salt, and stir for a minute. Add the ground cumin and 1 tbsp boiling water. Cover and cook the spiced potato mixture over a low to medium heat for 4 minutes. Stir in the tomato and sugar, if using. Wash the rice flakes in cold water and strain. Add the flakes to the pan and stir for a minute. Cover and cook over a low heat for a further 8-10 minutes until the potatoes are tender. If you're not serving this with yogurt, add 1 tbsp lemon juice. Garnish with the coriander leaves and desiccated coconut. Serve hot with yogurt.

Crisp, spicy, and fried Gujarati snacks can be bought from shops and wayside stalls everywhere and are called "farsans" throughout India. *Chai* or tea is usually served with them. This particular snack is prepared for all festivals, but especially around August to September, during the festival of Ganesh, the elephant god, revered throughout India but particularly in the West.

chivda
चिवड़ा
savoury rice flakes

serves 6

vegetable oil, for deep-frying

300g (10½oz) rice flakes

30g (1oz) whole unsalted cashew nuts

½ tsp brown or black mustard seeds

½ tsp cumin seeds

pinch of asafoetida (optional)

¼ tsp turmeric

2–3 green finger chillies, finely chopped

1tsp salt

115g (4oz) Bombay mix

1tsp granulated sugar

30g (1oz) sultanas

Heat the oil for deep-frying to 180°C/350°F. Add a few rice flakes to the oil; if they sizzle and rise to the surface, the oil is ready. Add the rice flakes in batches of about 5tbsp and deep-fry for 15–20 seconds or until golden, then remove them from the oil immediately with a slotted spoon. Place on kitchen paper to absorb the oil. This process takes about 10 minutes. Put the fried rice flakes in a bowl. In the same oil, fry the cashew nuts for a minute until golden brown, then remove, drain on kitchen paper and add to the rice flakes.

In a separate pan, heat 2tbsp oil and add the mustard and cumin seeds, asafoetida, if using, turmeric, chillies, and salt. Mix into the rice flake mixture. Add the Bombay mix, sugar, and sultanas. Mix thoroughly. Allow to cool and store in an airtight container for up to 3 months. Serve with *panna* (see page 253) or tea made with *chai ka masala* (see page 199).

Puffed rice is the essence of many dishes sold by the road or on the beaches of Mumbai (Bombay), the capital of Maharashtra. It's mainly used for snacks like *bhelpuri*, a mixture of puffed rice, chutneys, and nuts. It's an acquired taste – sweet, salty, sour, and hot – delicious. The chutneys can be stored for up to 4 days in the refrigerator.

bhelpuri
भेलपुरि
puffed rice with date and tamarind chutney

for the date and tamarind chutney:
50g (1¾oz) dried dates, stoned and
  chopped
1tbsp tamarind concentrate

¼tsp salt
¼tsp medium-hot chilli powder
1tsp vegetable or groundnut oil
30g (1oz) dark muscovado sugar

In a blender, blitz all the ingredients to a fairly smooth paste with 4tbsp cold water.

for the green chutney:
30g (1oz) coriander leaves, chopped
4 green finger chillies, roughly chopped
1 garlic clove, crushed

1tsp peeled and finely grated root
  ginger
4 mint leaves (optional)
¼tsp salt

In a blender, blitz all the ingredients to a smooth paste with 4tbsp cold water.

for the bhelpuri:
155g (5½oz) puffed rice
1 medium white onion, finely chopped
200g (7oz) white or red potatoes,
  boiled and cut in 2cm (⅘ inch) cubes

1 medium tomato, chopped
20g (¾oz) coriander leaves, finely
  chopped, plus extra to serve
155g (5½oz) Bombay mix or *chivda*
5–6 *pooris* or tortilla chips, broken

Mix all the ingredients together. Serve 3–4tbsp of *bhelpuri* with 1tsp of each of the chutneys on top. Sprinkle with more coriander and serve with yogurt.

The word *"bhaji"* means "vegetables" in West India, and there's an enormous variety of vegetables available here. Hinduism demands purity of mind and spirit, and a vegetarian diet, so there's an unlimited and imaginative variety of vegetarian fare. Many vegetable combinations can be used in this recipe.

sukhi bhaji
सुखी भाजी
dry vegetable curry

serves 2–3

2tbsp vegetable or groundnut oil

1 medium white onion, finely chopped

200g (7oz) courgettes, cut into 2.5cm (1 inch) cubes

100g (3¾oz) white potatoes, peeled and cut into 2.5cm (1 inch) cubes

50g (1¾oz) peas

¼ tsp salt

2tsp Maharashtrian masala (page 236)

1tsp peeled and finely grated root ginger

1tbsp skinned peanuts, roasted and crushed

Heat the oil in a heavy-based pan and add the onion. Gently fry for 5 minutes. Add the courgettes, potatoes, and peas. Mix for a minute, then add the salt and Maharashtrian *masala*. Fry for 3 minutes over a medium heat. Pour in 300ml (10½ oz) boiling water. Cover and simmer on a low heat for 20 minutes or until the vegetables are tender. Stir in the ginger and sprinkle over the crushed peanuts. Serve hot with *chapatis* and *chawlichi bhaji* (see page 206).

Maharashtrians call curry, or any dish with a sauce base, *kaalvan*. The interesting thing about this curry is that it has no onions; the flavours come from the simple mixture of spices. This salmon curry is delicious served with *chawal basmati* (see page 54) and a salad.

kaalvan
कालवन
marathi salmon curry

serves 2–3

2tbsp groundnut or vegetable oil

2–3 garlic cloves, slightly crushed

255g (9oz) skinned and boned
  salmon steaks

1tsp rice flour or plain flour

1tsp hot chilli powder

½tsp turmeric

1tsp ground cumin

1tsp ground coriander

½tsp salt

½tsp tamarind concentrate

200ml (7fl oz) coconut milk

Heat the oil in a heavy-based pan. Add the garlic and fish. Fry each side of the steaks over a low heat for 4-5 minutes until lightly browned. In a bowl, mix together all the other ingredients, except the coconut milk, with 155ml (5½fl oz) cold water. Add to the pan and simmer for 3 minutes. Mix the coconut milk with 100ml (3½fl oz) boiling water and add to the pan, cover and simmer for 7 minutes: the sauce should be runny. Serve hot with *chawlichi bhaji* (see page 206).

Maharashtrian cuisine includes subtly flavoured vegetarian delicacies, but it also contains hot and aromatic meat and fish curries. The seafood-based Konkani and Malwani cuisines come from the region's coast. *Kolambi masala* is a deliciously spiced and fiery thin sauce with prawns, that is served as part of a main meal at lunchtime or in the evening. The prawns are shelled while eating.

kolambi masala
कोलम्बी मसाला
spiced prawn

serves 2–3

2 tbsp vegetable oil

½ medium white onion, finely chopped

3 garlic cloves, crushed

2 green finger chillies, finely chopped, or ¼ tsp hot chilli powder

15–20 raw prawns with shells

½ tsp tamarind paste

pinch of asafoetida (optional)

¼ tsp salt

1 tsp ground cumin

½ tsp turmeric

1 tsp ground coriander

200ml (7fl oz) coconut milk

handful of coriander leaves, roughly chopped

Heat the oil in a heavy-based pan or wok. Gently fry the onion, garlic, and green chillies, if using, for 2 minutes until the onion looks glazed. Add the prawns and stir-fry for 2 minutes. Remove from the heat.

Mix the tamarind paste with 2tbsp cold water and leave for 2 minutes. In a small bowl, mix together the asafoetida and chilli powder, if using, salt, cumin, turmeric, and ground coriander, with 2tbsp cold water. Add this mixture to the prawns and stir for a minute. Stir the diluted tamarind into the prawn mixture with 255ml (9fl oz) boiling water. Simmer for 2 minutes, then add the coconut milk. Gently simmer for 6–8 minutes, but do not boil. Garnish with coriander leaves and serve with *basmati chawal* (see page 54) and a mixed vegetable curry. Shell the prawns when eating.

Balchao de camarao is a Goan recipe in which the prawns are cooked in a brine sauce. Often vegetables such as aubergines are also "pickled" in sugar, vinegar, and spices for a day or two before eating. The tangier the better.

balchao de camarao
बालचाओ दी कामाराओ
pickled prawns

serves 2–3

2tsp peeled and finely grated root ginger

2 garlic cloves, roughly chopped

4 dried medium red chillies, stalks removed

1tbsp malt vinegar

2 cloves

¼tsp brown or black mustard seeds or ¼tsp mustard powder (optional)

½tsp ground cumin

¼tsp salt

¼tsp ground cinnamon

½tsp turmeric

2tbsp groundnut oil or vegetable oil

170g (6oz) raw king prawns, shelled and de-veined

4–6 curry leaves

1 small white onion, finely chopped

2 medium tomatoes, finely chopped

Mince the ginger, garlic, chillies, vinegar, cloves, mustard seeds or powder, cumin, salt, ground cinnamon, and turmeric to a fairly smooth paste in a food processor. Heat 1tbsp oil in a wok or a saucepan and sauté the prawns for 5 minutes until all the water has evaporated. Remove the prawns with a slotted spoon, drain on kitchen paper and set aside. In the same pan, add 1tbsp oil followed by the curry leaves. Stir in the onion and fry over a medium heat for 6 minutes until golden.

Add the tomatoes to the fried onions and cook for about 2 minutes. Stir in the ginger paste and gently fry for 2 minutes. Add 2tbsp cold water to the blender to rinse and add this water to the pan. Return the prawns to the pan and simmer for a further 3 minutes. Serve hot or cold sprinkled with a pinch of chilli powder.

This curry is usually made for special occasions, such as weddings and festivals. It's a popular Parsee dish of chicken served with potato straws: traditionally julienne potatoes deep-fried in oil.

sali margi
साली मर्गी
spicy chicken curry

serves 2-3

vegetable oil, for deep-frying

200g (7oz) white potatoes, peeled

2 garlic cloves, roughly chopped

1tsp peeled and grated root ginger

½tsp each ground cinnamon, ground cumin, and turmeric

¼tsp *garam masala*

2 green finger chillies, chopped

2tbsp vegetable oil

2 Spanish onions, finely chopped

2tsp tomato purée

500g (1lb 2oz) boneless, skinless chicken breasts, in 4cm (1½ inch) cubes

½tsp salt

2tsp lemon juice

Heat the oil to 180°C/350°F in a wok. Coarsely grate the potatoes to make thin strips. Place them on kitchen paper and squeeze out any excess water. To check the oil is hot enough, add a potato strip; if it sizzles, the oil is ready. Fry the potatoes for 2½ minutes until they are golden. Drain on kitchen paper and cool.

Blitz the garlic, ginger, cinnamon, cumin, turmeric, *garam masala*, and green chillies with 2tbsp cold water in a blender until it forms a smooth paste, or use a pestle and mortar. Heat the oil in a wok or heavy-based pan and fry the onions over a low heat for 10 minutes or until golden. Add the garlic paste, then the tomato purée, and mix for a minute. Tip in the chicken and salt and fry for 5–6 minutes. Rinse out the blender or mortar with 200ml (7fl oz) boiling water and pour this into the pan with the chicken. Simmer for 7 minutes, until the chicken is cooked through. Sprinkle the lemon juice and potato sticks over the chicken.

Galinha cafreal has been described as tandoori chicken's Goan cousin. It's essentially a whole or jointed chicken marinated in chillies, vinegar or lime juice, and spices. The chicken can be deep-fried, barbecued or roasted.

galinha cafreal
गोलिन्हा कफरील
barbecued chicken

serves 4

1kg (2lb 3oz) skinless chicken thighs and legs

juice of 1 lime

¾ tsp salt

4 dried large red or Kashmiri chillies, stalks removed

1 green finger chilli, roughly chopped

4 black peppercorns

3 tsp coriander seeds

1 tsp peeled and finely grated root ginger

4 cloves garlic, roughly chopped

2cm (⅘ inch) mace blade (optional)

1 x 2.5cm (1 inch) cinnamon stick or cassia bark

2 tbsp vegetable oil

1 tbsp malt vinegar

½ medium white onion

Preheat the oven to 180°C/350°F/gas mark 4. Prick the chicken pieces all over with a fork. Mix 1tbsp lime juice and ½tsp salt and rub on to the chicken. In a blender, or with a pestle and mortar, blitz the red and green chillies, peppercorns, coriander, ginger, garlic, mace, if using, cinnamon, 1tbsp of the oil, the remaining salt, vinegar, and onion into a runny paste.

Rub the paste into the chicken, cover and refrigerate for 30 minutes. Place the chicken in a single layer in a roasting tin and smother with the leftover marinade. Cover with foil and place in the centre of the oven. Roast for 65 minutes, or until cooked through, basting twice during cooking with 1tbsp oil. Rest the meat for 15 minutes. Serve with *theplas* (see page 231) and *Goan salada* (see page 209).

Parsee food is an amalgamation of many cooking techniques. Though it's not chilli-hot, it is rich and spicy and as varied as the food found in any other region. Parsees are primarily non-vegetarian and particularly enjoy eating chicken and mutton, as well as eggs. This dish is a favourite snack and party food. Pieces of chicken are marinated in a spicy paste, dipped in breadcrumbs and beaten egg, then deep-fried.

margi nu farcha
मगी नू फारचा
parsee fried chicken

serves 2–3

vegetable oil, for deep-frying

¼tsp medium chilli powder

¼tsp salt

¼tsp ground cumin

¼tsp ground coriander

1tsp peeled and finely grated root ginger (optional)

1 garlic clove, crushed

1tsp malt vinegar

1tsp demerara sugar

400g (14oz) skinless chicken fillets, cut in 4cm (1⅗inch) long strips

2 medium eggs

4tbsp dried coarse white breadcrumbs

In a large bowl, mix 1tbsp oil, the chilli powder, salt, cumin, coriander, ginger, if using, garlic, vinegar, and sugar. Add the chicken pieces and stir to coat thoroughly. Cover and refrigerate for 3 hours or overnight.

Heat the oil to 180°C/350°F. Add a droplet of egg; if it sizzles and rises to the surface, the oil is ready. Beat the eggs. Spread the breadcrumbs on a large plate. Dip the chicken in the egg, then in the breadcrumbs, coating evenly. Fry in batches for about 10 minutes or until cooked and golden.

When I think of Goa, I think of long, warm, sunny days on tranquil beaches and, of course, the food. Many restaurant menus include a *xacuti* dish. Pronounced "shaguti", this sauce is made with coconut, red chillies, tamarind, and an aromatic blend of spices. *Xacuti* is usually prepared with chicken, but there are variations with beef.

galinha xacuti
गेलिन्हा जाकुटि
chicken in an aromatic coconut sauce

serves 2–3

4 black peppercorns

4 cloves

1 star anise

1tsp fennel seeds (optional)

3 dried red chillies, stalks removed

3 green cardamoms

½ tsp poppy seeds

2 x 2.5cm (1 inch) cinnamon sticks

¼ tsp salt

¼ tsp turmeric

½ tsp ground cumin

¼ tsp ground coriander

2tbsp groundnut oil

1 medium white onion, finely chopped

1 garlic clove, finely chopped

400g (14oz) boneless chicken thighs
 and drumsticks

200ml (7fl oz) coconut milk

¼ tsp tamarind concentrate

Heat a frying pan and add the peppercorns, cloves, star anise, fennel seeds, if using, red chillies, cardamoms, poppy seeds, and cinnamon, and roast for a minute. Put the roasted spices in a coffee mill with the salt, turmeric, cumin, and coriander and grind to a coarse powder. Alternatively, use a pestle and mortar.

Heat the oil in a pan and fry the onion and garlic for 3 minutes. Add the chicken pieces and sauté for 6–7 minutes, browning them all over. Add the ground spice mixture and stir-fry for a minute, then add 100ml (3½fl oz) boiling water, and simmer for 5 minutes. Mix the coconut milk with 200ml (7fl oz) boiling water, then add to the chicken and simmer for another 6 minutes. Stir in the tamarind and cook for another 5–7 minutes, until it reaches the consistency of runny gravy and the chicken is cooked through. Sprinkle with grated coconut and serve.

Chicken is called *"kombdi"* in the state of Maharashtra, where non-vegetarian curries are made with an abundance of chilli and *garam masala*, giving them the fullest flavour. This recipe comes from the town of Kolhapur, a good place to sample meat specialities.

sukhi kombdi
सुखी कोम्बडी
dry chicken

serves 2–3

3 tbsp groundnut oil

1 medium white onion, finely chopped

2 garlic cloves, finely chopped

1 tsp peeled and finely grated root ginger

1 tsp *garam masala*

1 tsp hot chilli powder

½ tsp turmeric

¼ tsp salt

2 medium tomatoes, finely chopped

500g (1lb 2oz) boneless and skinless chicken breasts, cut into 5cm (2 inch) chunks

1 tbsp desiccated coconut

1 tbsp lemon juice

1 tsp chopped coriander leaves

Heat the oil in a heavy-based pan and gently fry the onion, garlic and ginger for 10 minutes until light golden. Add the *garam masala*, chilli powder, turmeric, and salt and fry for 1 minute. Add the tomatoes and stir-fry for 2 minutes. Tip in the chicken chunks and coconut and fry over a medium heat for 5 minutes. Add 155ml (5½fl oz) boiling water.

Cover and simmer for 12 minutes, or until the chicken is cooked through. Stir in the lemon juice and sprinkle over the coriander leaves. Serve hot with *chapatis* or *fodnicha bhaat* (see page 230).

Use freshly cooked rice for this dish, but allow it to cool down before use by spreading it out on a plate. 200g (7oz) uncooked white rice will yield approximately 400g (14oz) cooked rice.

fodnicha bhaat
फोदनिचा भात
spiced rice

serves 2–3

2tbsp vegetable oil
1tsp each salt and cumin seeds
¼tsp brown mustard seeds
1 white onion, finely sliced
2 green finger chillies, chopped
½tsp turmeric powder
400g (14oz) freshly cooked white rice

Heat the oil in a heavy-based pan or wok, then add the cumin and mustard seeds. When they pop and sizzle, tip in the onion and fry for 4 minutes or until the onion is soft and glazed. Add the chillies and stir for a minute, then add the turmeric and salt. Finally add the rice and mix thoroughly. Serve piping hot with *kolambi masala* (see page 221).

Theplas are Gujarati baked flatbreads, and are similar to *chapatis*. The dough is made with wheat flour, often mixed with chickpea flour, and fresh fenugreek leaves. Many Gujaratis avoid eating garlic for religious reasons, so there are very few recipes from the region that contain it.

theplas
थेपला
unleavened fenugreek flatbreads

makes 5–6 *theplas*

150g (5¼oz) wholewheat flour, plus extra for dusting

¼ tsp turmeric

pinch of asafoetida (optional)

20–30g (¾–1oz) fenugreek leaves, finely chopped, or 2tbsp dried

½ tsp mild chilli powder

½ tsp ground coriander

½ tsp cumin seeds

¼ tsp peeled and finely grated root ginger

3tbsp vegetable or groundnut oil

Mix together the flour, turmeric, asafoetida, if using, fenugreek leaves, chilli powder, coriander, cumin, ginger, and 1tbsp of the oil, then add approximately 100ml (3½floz) tepid water and knead the mixture for 5–7 minutes into a soft pliable dough. Leave covered for 10–15 minutes.

Divide the dough into 6 equal-sized balls. Cover them with a damp cloth while you are working to stop the dough drying out. Take each ball and, with a dusting of flour, roll it out into 12.5cm (5½ inch) discs, about 2mm (¹⁄₁₀ inch) thick. Heat a griddle. When it is hot, add 1tsp of the oil and place a disc on to the griddle. Cook for about 1½ minutes on each side, carefully pressing the disc firmly down so that all the *thepla* is cooked. Cover with foil and place in a warm oven while you cook the remaining discs, adding 1tsp oil each time. Serve hot with *sukhlele vangyachi chatni* (see page 239) and a mixed vegetable curry.

Recheio spice paste is a wet mixture of fresh and dried spices combined with vinegar. The Portuguese 400-year occupation left Goan cuisine a legacy of unusual colonial and culinary traditions. *Recheio* spice paste includes vinegar as a souring agent that is unique to this region. The paste mixture is primarily used for making Goan pork *vindaloo* and Goan sausages called *chouricos*. *Recheio* spice paste makes a great marinade for fish and chicken.

recheio

रेंकियो मसाला पेस्ट

recheio spice paste

makes 5tbsp

6 medium dried red chillies, stalks removed

1tsp cumin seeds

6–8 black peppercorns

1tsp turmeric

½ small Spanish or white onion, finely chopped (optional)

2tsp peeled and finely grated root ginger

6 garlic cloves, roughly chopped

1tsp tamarind concentrate

1tsp demerara sugar

½tsp salt

2tbsp malt vinegar

Rinse and soak the chillies in 3tbsp boiling water for 5 minutes, place the chillies and their soaking water with the rest of the ingredients in a blender and blitz for 2 minutes or until they form a smooth paste. Alternatively, use a pestle and mortar. Store in an airtight, non-metallic container in the refrigerator for up to 5 days.

2tsp *recheio* spice paste serves 4 people: after frying the onions for the recipe in oil, add the paste and, on a low heat, fry for a minute. Add the vegetables or meat and cook.

This dark brown spice mixture is very common in Maharashtrian cuisine, imparting a fiery flavour to many recipes that originate from this state. This *masala* is just like the North's *garam masala* and is extremely versatile. Just use 1tsp per person in a meat, chicken or fish curry.

maharashtrian masala
मराठी मसाला
marathi spice mix

makes approx 3tbsp

1tbsp coriander seeds

1tsp fennel seeds

1tsp poppy seeds (optional)

1tsp black caraway seeds or black cumin seeds

6 x 4cm (1⅗ inch) cinnamon sticks

6 cloves

10 black peppercorns

1tsp ground mace (optional)

8 green cardamoms, seeds only

5 black cardamoms, seeds only

10 dried medium red chillies, stalks removed

1tsp turmeric

generous pinch of asafoetida

Heat a frying pan and roast all the ingredients, except the turmeric and asafoetida, for 2 minutes, making sure they don't burn. Place the turmeric, asafoetida and roasted spices in a blender. Blitz to a fine powder. Alternatively, use a pestle and mortar. Store the mixture in an airtight container in a cool, dark place for up to 8 months.

"Koshimbir" in Marathi means salad. Indians tend not to make elaborate dressings that include oil. This is a quick salad with a simple dressing of lemon juice and salt, the main flavours coming from the chilli and the coriander.

mooli chi koshimbir
मूलीची कोशिम्बीर
maharashtrian radish salad

serves 2–3

155g (5½oz) radishes, topped and tailed

1 small white onion, finely chopped

½tsp salt

1 green finger chilli, finely chopped

2 medium tomatoes, finely chopped

2tsp lemon juice

30g (1oz) coriander leaves, roughly chopped

Coarsely grate the radishes and mix with the rest of the ingredients. Serve as a fresh relish with any fish curry, such as *kaalvan* (see page 218), mixed vegetable curry and *kolambi masala* (see page 221).

This chutney is delicious simply accompanied by *theplas* (see page 231).
It has quite a mild flavour.

sukhlele vangyachi chatni
सुखलेले वांगयाची चटनी
aubergine chutney

serves 4

1tsp salt

1 large aubergine, cut into 2.5cm (1 inch) cubes

1tbsp groundnut oil

pinch of asafoetida

2 green finger chillies, roughly chopped

2 garlic cloves, roughly chopped

½ tsp ground cumin

1tsp tamarind concentrate

a few sprigs coriander, leaves only

Sprinkle the salt over the aubergine cubes and set aside for 10 minutes. Rinse with cold water and then squeeze out the water and remove the most obvious seeds. Blot dry with kitchen paper. Heat the oil in a heavy-based pan. Add the asafoetida and mix for a few seconds, followed by the aubergine. Sauté for a minute and then add the chillies, garlic, and cumin. Stir in the tamarind concentrate. Gently cook for 2 minute, or until the aubergine is tender. Mix in the coriander leaves. Leave to cool for a few minutes and then place in a blender. Alternatively, use a pestle and mortar. Blitz until the mixture becomes a rough paste.

The abundant use of peanuts in Maharashtrian and Gujarati cooking has led to countless recipes that use them in street food, elaborate meals, and sweets. This chutney is a spicy, rough mixture that usually accompanies vegetables and rice.

shengdaniachi chatni
शेंगडानियाची चटनी
peanut chutney

serves 4

100g (3¾oz) unsalted peanuts
¼ tsp each hot chilli powder and salt
½ tsp ground cumin
pinch of asafoetida (optional)

Using a blender or pestle and mortar, grind all the ingredients together into a coarse paste. This can be stored in an airtight, non-metallic container in the refrigerator for up to a week.

Before convenience foods became the norm, Indian women were recognized for their expertise in preparing pickles – the most popular kind of preserve. There are literally hundreds of pickle recipes using almost every fruit and vegetable under the sun. No Indian meal is complete without pickle.

aam ka achar
आम का अचार
quick mango pickle

makes 20 servings
**600g (1lb 5oz) raw green
  mangoes, peeled**
4tbsp vegetable oil
1tsp brown mustard seeds
½ tsp turmeric
2tsp hot chilli powder
½ tsp salt
4tsp demerara sugar

Peel and stone the mangoes. Cut into 1cm (⅖ inch) cubes. Heat the oil in a pan and tip in the mustard seeds. When they begin to splutter, add the turmeric followed by the mangoes, chilli powder, salt, and sugar. Stir over a low heat for 4 minutes. Cool. Store in an airtight non-metallic container in the refrigerator for up to a week. Use as a relish with a main meal of mild dishes.

The Portuguese influence in Goa is particularly evident at Christmas. One of the seasonal dishes is the "queen of Goan desserts" – the celebrated *bebinca*. Although it's associated with Christmas, this eight-layered dessert, made of eggs, coconut milk, and sugar, is sold every morning in certain areas, just like fresh bread.

bebinca
बेबिंका
goanese cake

serves 6–8

100g (3¾oz) unsalted butter, plus extra for greasing

400ml (14fl oz) coconut milk

300g (10½oz) granulated sugar

10 large egg yolks, beaten

200g (7oz) plain white flour, sifted

¼ tsp freshly grated nutmeg

4 green cardamoms, seeds only, crushed

icing sugar, to serve

Preheat the oven to 180°C/350°F/gas mark 4. Butter a 16cm (6½ inch) round cake tin or line it with greaseproof paper. Place the coconut milk in a pan over a low heat. Gradually add the sugar, stirring constantly until it has dissolved. Take the pan off the heat and mix in the egg yolks a little at a time, stirring constantly. Gradually stir the flour, nutmeg, and cardamom to make a runny batter.

Melt the butter and spoon 1tbsp into the cake tin. Pour about 115ml (4fl oz) of the batter into the tin and bake for 10 minutes until golden. Remove from the oven, then add 2tbsp melted butter, followed by another 115ml (4fl oz) batter. Return the tin to the oven for a further 10 minutes until golden. Repeat this process until all the batter is used up in the final layer. Bake for 30 minutes or until the surface is golden brown. Allow to cool in the tin. Remove from the tin and chill. Sprinkle a thin layer of icing sugar over the top and cut into 1cm (⅖ inch) thick slices. Serve with whipped cream.

Jaggery is a dark, coarse, unrefined sugar made by boiling the sap of the palm tree. Jaggery imparts a sweet and wine-like fragrance. It is also sometimes referred to as "palm sugar". Primarily used in India as a sweetening agent, it comes in several forms, the two most popular being one with a soft, honey-butter texture and another in a solid cake-like form. The former is used to spread on breads, while the latter is used for sweets such as *chikki*.

shengdaniachi chikki
शेंगदानीआची चिक्की
indian peanut brittle

serves 4

1tsp unsalted butter
100g (3¾oz) brown jaggery or muscovado sugar
100g (3¾oz) unsalted shelled peanuts, crushed

Butter a large plate and set aside. Heat a small heavy-based pan and add the jaggery with 1tbsp cold water. Stir for 10 minutes or until the jaggery has completely dissolved and begins to bubble. Take the pan off the heat and tip in the peanuts. Mix for a few seconds coating all the peanuts in the sugar. Carefully and quickly pour the thick mixture on to the greased plate before it hardens. Spread the mixture evenly over the plate and leave to cool. Break into bite-size pieces and serve. Store for up to 4 weeks in an airtight container.

The Parsee community is confined mostly to the states of Maharashtra and Gujarat. Their festivals are quiet affairs compared to those of other communities in India, and opulence is only demonstrated through the associated feasts, which would include dishes such as *patra ni machchi* (fish steamed in a banana leaf), *margi nu farcha* (fried chicken), *sali boti* (lamb in a sweet and sour sauce sprinkled with potato crisps or thin straws), *mawa ni boi* (milk dessert laced with nuts), and *lagan nu custard*.

lagan nu custard
लगन नू कस्टर्ड
wedding custard

serves 4

155g (5½oz) caster sugar

710ml (25fl oz) full-fat milk

3 medium eggs

1tsp vanilla essence

1tsp rose water or *kewra* (optional)

8 green cardamoms, seeds only, crushed

¼tsp freshly grated nutmeg

15 unblanched almonds, sliced

whipped cream, to serve

In a heavy-based pan, dissolve the sugar in the milk, stirring occasionally, then simmer for half an hour on a low heat until the mixture has reduced by almost half. Leave to cool.

Preheat the oven to 180°C/350°F/gas mark 4. In a bowl, whisk the eggs with the vanilla essence, rose water or *kewra*, if using, cardamoms, and nutmeg. Add to the cooled milk mixture and stir. Pour into a 15cm (6 inch) flan dish, sprinkle the almonds on top, and bake for 40 minutes or until the top is golden brown. Remove from the oven and leave to cool. Refrigerate for at least 40 minutes. Slice and serve with whipped cream.

Semolina is known as *"rava"* or *"sooji"* in Hindi. It is the basis for many Indian sweets served during prayers or a *Puja* (ritual time to honour a specific deity). *Puja* is carried out during an auspicious occasion such as after a wedding. The semolina dish is prepared, blessed, and then offered as *prasad* (a sacred offering).

puja sheera
पूजा शीरा
semolina dessert

serves 4

2 green cardamoms, seeds only

50g (1¾oz) unsalted butter or *ghee*

100g (3¾oz) semolina

100ml (3½fl oz) full-fat milk

50g (1¾oz) granulated or demerara sugar

1tsp runny honey

1 medium banana, roughly chopped

a few saffron strands

Crush the cardamom seeds with a pestle and mortar and set aside. Melt the butter or *ghee* in a heavy-based pan and add the semolina. Cook for 5 minutes, stirring constantly. Stir in 200ml (7fl oz) boiling water, followed by the milk, cardamom seeds, sugar, and honey. Cook for 2 minutes. Add the banana and the saffron. Mix well and serve immediately.

Indians love to spice things up and that includes anything sweet. I discovered this drink on the coast of Mumbai, where there were plenty of eateries serving spicy milkshakes and chilli-flavoured ice cream, which believe me are an acquired taste! The combination of cold and chilli-hot sensations make sense because if you need to kill the heat of a spicy dish you drink milk or eat yogurt.

masala doodh
मसाला दूध
chilli hot chocolate

serves 2

50g (1¾oz) 70% dark chocolate

10tsp single cream

10tsp full-fat milk

50g (1¾oz) drinking chocolate powder

¼tsp ground cinnamon

30g (1oz) demerara sugar

1 dried medium red chilli, stalk removed

chilli flakes, to serve

Break the chocolate into small pieces and place in a small heavy-based pan with all the other ingredients. Simmer gently for 5 minutes, whisking occasionally, until the chocolate has dissolved. Strain the mixture through a nylon sieve and serve immediately in small espresso cups sprinkled with a few chilli flakes and chocolate gratings.

A refreshing and cooling drink that is served during the summer months when green mangoes are in season.

panna
पन्ना
green mango juice

serves 2

310g (11oz) green mangoes
pinch of salt
4tsp demerara sugar
2 green cardamoms
mint sprigs, to serve

Wash the mangoes, then boil for 20 minutes or until the mango skin becomes very soft. Carefully remove from the water. Leave to cool. Squeeze the mango flesh away from the skin and stones and place in a heavy-based pan with 710ml (25fl oz) cold water, the salt, sugar, and cardamoms. Cover and simmer for 10 minutes. Pour the mixture through a nylon sieve and discard the spices and pulp fibres. Serve chilled with a sprig of mint.

Few drinks – if any – are served with traditional meals in India. Water is the most common, but under the influence of the West and MTV culture, consuming cold drinks with a meal is becoming popular and fashionable. Wine is still rare in India – beer and whisky are the most popular alcoholic choices.

ananas sharbat
अनानास पंच
pineapple punch

serves 2

255ml (9fl oz) fresh
 pineapple juice
1 x 2cm (⅘ inch) cinnamon stick
2 green cardamoms
2 cloves
3–4 mint leaves (optional)
vodka (optional)

In a small, heavy-based pan bring half the pineapple juice to the boil with the cinnamon, cardamoms, cloves and mint leaves, if using. Cover the pan and simmer gently for 10 minutes. Cool the mixture, strain and add the remaining pineapple juice. Serve chilled with a dash of vodka, if using.

index

Acknowledgements

A big thank you to my mum, Kami, my brother Meno, Werner
Van Peppen and Khazina Khan. Abha, Bill and Sean Adams. Jo
and Nick Barrett, Pauline Barrett, Robin Barrett and Joyce Robins.
   Amit and Namita Bhatia, Girja Shanker, Sharupa Dutta, Bhairavi
Patel, Isky and Amu, Premchand and Latha, Nimmy and Paul
Variamparambil, B. Srinivasan, Sanjoy Roy, Shailan Parker, Jaideep
and Seema Mehrotra, Anne Richardson, Arvinder Suri, Aruna,
Rashmi Kao, Jamal Hirani, Nicola Pheonix, Rachael Robertson,
Neil Sexton, Ian Barclay, Dan McEvoy, Terry Wilson, Karen Deco
and Meriam Soopee. Jamal Hirani, Jill Franklin, Jane Opoku,
Sunita Verma, John Mwale, Michele Fisher, Pedro Carvalho,

Karen Bans, Navdeep and Mani Suri, Sonu and Lia P Lalvani,
Raj Ghatak, Stephen Rahman, Shailan Parker, Sanjoy Roy,
Dr Roopa Patel, Richard Kenney, Navdip Dhariwal and Mark at
seasonedpioneers.co.uk
   Becca Spry, Jason Lowe, Miranda Harvey, Yasia Williams,
Sunil Vijayakar, Fiona Smith, Jane Aspden, Mark Scott and
Diona Gregory.
   Mary Jones, Martine Carter and Michelle Wadsley.
   Please visit my website **www.manjumalhi.com** and you can
visit **www.seasonedpioneers.co.uk** if you need unusual spices
which you cannot find in your local shops.